Y0-BNP-269

TEMPERAMENT-BASED ELEMENTARY CLASSROOM MANAGEMENT

TEMPERAMENT-BASED ELEMENTARY CLASSROOM MANAGEMENT

SANDEE GRAHAM McCLOWRY

ROWMAN & LITTLEFIELD
Lanham • Boulder • New York • Toronto • Plymouth, UK

Published by Rowman & Littlefield
4501 Forbes Boulevard, Suite 200, Lanham, Maryland 20706
www.rowman.com

10 Thornbury Road, Plymouth PL6 7PP, United Kingdom

Copyright © 2014 by Sandee Graham McClowry

All rights reserved. No part of this book may be reproduced in any form or by any electronic or mechanical means, including information storage and retrieval systems, without written permission from the publisher, except by a reviewer who may quote passages in a review.

British Library Cataloguing in Publication Information Available

Library of Congress Cataloging-in-Publication Data

McClowry, Sandee Graham.
  Temperament-based elementary classroom management / Sandee Graham McClowry.
    pages cm
  Includes bibliographical references and index.
  ISBN 978-1-4758-0942-8 (cloth : alk. paper)—ISBN 978-1-4758-0943-5 (pbk. : alk. paper)—ISBN 978-1-4758-0944-2 (electronic) 1. Classroom management. 2. Education, Elementary. 3. Temperament in children. 4. Individual differences in children. I. Title.
  LB3013.M3817 2014
  371.102'4—dc23   2014003640

♾™ The paper used in this publication meets the minimum requirements of American National Standard for Information Sciences—Permanence of Paper for Printed Library Materials, ANSI/NISO Z39.48-1992.

Printed in the United States of America

CONTENTS

THE 3 Rs OF TEMPERAMENT-BASED CLASSROOM MANAGEMENT—RECOGNIZE, REFRAME, AND RESPOND

CLASSROOMS are a conglomerate of diverse individuals with a united goal: educating their student members. Teachers who are effective in their role as educators provide their students with an environment conducive to learning. In other words, classroom management is critical if students are to learn and for educators to teach.

Most teachers appreciate that their students have different learning styles. Another characteristic that varies among students is their temperament, which is often referred to as personality. Understanding how children differ in their temperaments assists teachers in supporting the academic and social-emotional development of their students. Teachers who understand children's temperament also know how to modify their classroom management strategies to match their students' temperaments.

The content for this book is based on an evidence-based intervention called *INSIGHTS into Children's Temperament*. The efficacy of *INSIGHTS* has been tested in three clinical trials. The content of the intervention and the results of the studies that examined its impact on students, teachers, and the children's parents will be presented throughout this book. As will be discussed, the teacher strategies derived from *INSIGHTS* support classroom management.

The first part of this book explains the 3 Rs of temperament-based classroom management: Recognize, Reframe, and Respond. Chapter 1 explains how to **recognize** student temperaments. Chapter 2 explores how **reframing** perceptions of students leads to the appreciation that no one temperament is ideal. Instead each temperament has strengths and issues that cause teachers concern. Chapter 3 focuses on teachers' **responses**. Multiple examples are presented in the chapter to demonstrate how teacher responses to students' behavior can alter the classroom environment and the relationship among the members of the classroom.

CHAPTER 1

RECOGNIZING CHILD TEMPERAMENT

OBSERVE any elementary school classroom and you will, more than likely, see some students who are industrious, others who are cautious, still others who are friendly, and a few who are high maintenance. Such individual characteristics can be attributed to a child's temperament. Understanding the temperament of children is posed in this book as a theoretical foundation for effective classroom management.

IN THIS CHAPTER:

- Temperament is defined.

- Six conclusions about elementary school–age children's temperament are explained.

- Theoretical frameworks that support temperament-based interventions are presented.

- Temperament-based classroom management is defined.

WHAT IS CHILD TEMPERAMENT?

Temperament is the consistent reaction style that a child demonstrates across a variety of settings and situations, particularly those that involve stress or change. The construct refers to an individual's emotional, attentional, and behavioral tendencies or dispositions (Rothbart & Bates, 2006). Temperament also is a social processing system through which children view and interact with the world, both altering the responses of others and contributing toward their own development.

As the scenario in box 1.1 demonstrates, children react to their first day in first grade in a variety of ways. The type and intensity of their responses are highly related

BOX 1.1. A CLASSROOM SCENARIO

The following scenario introduces you to four students, Hilary, Coretta, Freddy, and Gregory, each of whom has a distinctly different temperament. These children will be featured throughout this book to illustrate concepts related to temperament-based classroom management.

Today is the first day of school! For weeks, Ms. Davis has worked diligently preparing her first grade classroom. The bulletin boards are decorated with colorful welcome messages and packets of information are prepared for the children's parents.

Ms. Davis is standing by the door ready to welcome each of her students as they arrive. Their teacher last year, Mrs. Griffin, told her about the children. Ms. Davis easily recognizes the children as they arrive all dressed in their very best outfits. Among the students are the four who will be featured in this book:

Freddy has skillfully navigated close to Ms. Davis near the door. He also greets each of the kids who attended kindergarten last year by name. When Freddy sees someone who is new at the school, he smiles broadly and says, "Hi! I'm Freddy. What's your name?"

Hilary came into the classroom prepared. All of her school supplies are organized in her backpack. Hilary is delighted when she finds a desk with her name on it. She immediately begins to settle in.

Coretta seems to be near tears. She still is holding her mom's hand after all the other mothers have left.

Gregory tells Freddy that he would rather be playing baseball than be back at school. Even while grumbling, Gregory is distracted by all the excitement and activity going on in the classroom. After being directed to his desk, Gregory tries to sit down but his noble attempts are short-lived.

to their temperament. Note how they respond in a consistent way when they begin fifth grade.

This book is intended to enhance your classroom management skills by teaching you how to apply temperament-based strategies that are supported by scientific evidence. Recognizing the temperament of your students is a critical step in helping you establish and maintain a classroom that fosters emotional and academic development of your students. As Ms. Davis might say, "You are going to learn a great deal about child temperament in this book and it's going to be fun!"

An understanding of children's temperament is informed by a synthesis of literally thousands of temperament research studies. *PsychInfo*, an abstract database of psychological literature, lists more than 3,500 peer-reviewed articles and over 600 books that have been published on childhood temperament—just in the last ten years. The burgeoning literature is so large that it cannot be adequately presented in one chapter. Instead, research findings relevant to temperament of elementary students and their applications to classroom management will be introduced in this chapter and elaborated upon throughout this book.

Ms. Davis takes a deep breath and tells herself that it is going to be an exciting year. She smiles at the children and tells them that they are going to learn a great deal in first grade—and they are going to have a lot of fun!

The same four students appear in Ms. Jennings's classroom four years later on their first day in fifth grade:

The morning buzzer sounds and twenty-five fifth graders swarm into Ms. Jennings's room. The excitement of the students is palpable. Ms. Jennings greets each of them and refers them to a large seating plan posted at the front of the classroom.

Hilary breathes a sign of relief when she sees Ms. Jennings. She is happy that Ms. Jennings is her teacher this year. Her friend Sara was in Ms. Jennings's class last year. Sara said that Ms. Jennings made the class work really hard but that she was a really good teacher. Hilary is anticipating a great year.

Despite Sara's positive recommendation, Coretta tells Hilary she is not sure that she's going to like Ms. Jennings. She misses Mrs. Heather, her fourth grade teacher.

Freddy is wearing his signature baseball cap, which, this year, is twisted to the side. He has already made the rounds on the playground and has caught up with everyone's summertime stories.

Consistent with his attitude toward starting first grade, Gregory tells Freddy that he would rather be playing baseball than back at school.

After a great deal of flurry getting into their seats, Ms. Jennings begins: "Welcome, class, to fifth grade. I'm your teacher, Ms. Jennings."

MAJOR CONCLUSIONS ABOUT CHILD TEMPERAMENT

Knowledge about temperament has been derived from quantitative and qualitative research methodologies from a variety of disciplines. Given the diversity of disciplines who research temperament, it is no surprise that spirited debates occur on the best way to define and measure the construct (Shiner et al., 2012). Regardless of all the variations, six major conclusions about temperament are applicable to school-age children.

Temperament:

1. Is biologically based and resistant to change.
2. Predicts behavior.
3. Modulates one's perceptions of experiences.
4. Often is recognized in situations that involve change or stress.
5. Influences social interactions.
6. Classifies individuals.

Conclusion #1: Temperament is biologically based and resistant to change. Have you ever heard anyone say, *"It is his nature to be that way"*? When people remark about someone's nature, they imply that some characteristics of an individual are intrinsic and unlikely to change. Temperament is biologically based (Shiner et al., 2012). Babies are born with a particular temperament, although some infants take a few months before they consistently exhibit it.

Most parents become believers in temperament when a second child joins the family. Parents, who credited their parenting skills and the family environment for their first child's behavior, often rethink their stance when the new baby arrives. Feeding patterns or ways to comfort the first baby often are ineffective with the second infant.

Teachers have a similar experience when they have fraternal twins in their classroom. The twins may be very different from each other even though they are siblings who share much of the same family environment. Studies comparing identical twins with non-twin siblings show that genetics account for 20 to 60 percent of temperament with the remaining variability attributable to the environment (Saudino, 2005). The amount of heritability of temperament is not much different than intelligence, which is 48 percent (Deary, 2000).

Because of its biological basis, temperament is resistant to change. Adults should not try to overhaul a child's temperamental tendencies and dispositions. Insisting that a child behave in ways that are different from his or her temperament leads to frustration and is likely to be counterproductive. Such strategies undermine the child's self-esteem because they relay disapproval of his or her very nature. They also compromise the relationship between the adult and the child. This book is not intended to teach you strategies that change the temperament of your students. Instead, you will learn how to work *with* the student's temperament to enhance his or her development.

Sidebar 1.1. More about Temperament, Genetics, and the Environment

Recent advances in temperament research have provided additional insights into the complex interactions that occur over time between temperament, genetics, and the environment (Shiner et al., 2012). The interactions and their mutual effects begin before babies are born. Fetuses inherit genes from their parents that contribute to their temperamental dispositions. The uterine environment their mothers provide also affects the developing baby.

Some genes, especially those related to attention, become more influential during a child's development (Shiner et al., 2012). The environment also impacts a child's expression of their temperament. Some temperaments, compared to others, are more sensitive to the positive or negative aspects of their environments. Identifying individuals who are temperamentally at risk for maladaptation and altering the environment to support their development is the work of temperament-based intervention.

Conclusion #2: Temperament predicts behavior. Temperament is a composite of traits that are expressed by strong tendencies to demonstrate consistent, predictable behavior (Strelau, 2008). As you have probably observed, some students are always active and others are quiet most of the time. Or you may have noticed that some students tend to interpret any situation that involves waiting in line as an opportunity to socialize, while others complain relentlessly. Teachers are particularly aware of how students differ on attentional attributes. For some students, concentration comes very easy; others struggle with assignments that require focused attention.

Of course, all of your students will vary in their behavior to some degree. Even a child whose temperament is generally pleasant will have times when he or she is uncharacteristically grumpy. Anybody, even a little kid, can have a bad day! When we assess a child's temperament, however, we are looking for the child's *general* predisposition to exhibit a consistent behavioral style or pattern of behavior.

While temperament is relatively stable, its expression may gradually change over time due to maturation, experience, and the environment (Teglasi, 2006). For example, older children may differ in the intensity in which they express their temperament even though the underlying disposition is still present.

Conclusion #3: Temperament modulates one's perceptions of experiences. Although not as easily observable as their behavioral responses, temperament modulates how people perceive their experiences. Based on their temperament, individuals either augment or reduce their emotional response to an event (Strelau, 2008). Consequently, temperament contributes significantly to how they remember and interpret experiences. Surely, you have noticed that people often differ in their affective descriptions of the same event. Two students may describe an incident that occurred in the classroom and sound as if they had very different experiences. Indeed, they did!

Conclusion #4: Temperament is often recognized in situations that involve change or stress. Temperament is a powerful predictor of a student's reaction to change. Every day, multiple situations occur that are likely to elicit temperament reactions from your students. The classroom environment provides a myriad of experiences that students often regard as stressful. Classrooms introduce new people, situations, and academic content to students on an ongoing basis. Many circumstances, such as testing days, classroom visitors, multipart assignments, or working on a group project, provoke students to exhibit behavior indicative of their temperament. Disappointments, such as having to postpone a class outing because of inclement weather, are also distressful for many children. Change can be stressful even when it involves something positive like an upcoming vacation.

Students differ on the type of situations they find stressful. Some children find a quiet classroom boring, whereas other students are distressed by a great deal of noise. Everyone has an optimal level of arousal (Strelau, 2008). If a setting does not provide a comfortable level of arousal, an individual will try to alter it by making it more or less stimulating. For example, a student may initiate an activity or even mischief if he or she perceives the environment as dull or unexciting. Conversely another child, if surrounded with a great deal of noise or activity, may withdraw or at least try to minimize the stimulation by sitting in a quieter section of the classroom. Some children don't care whether there are negative consequences when they attempt to modify the environment; they simply are trying to get comfortable.

Conclusion #5: Temperament influences social interactions. Temperament influences the interactions students have with each other and with the adults in their lives, especially their teachers and parents. The reciprocity that occurs in these transactions has implications for future encounters. Children who are consistently pleasant are likely to elicit positive responses from others. Those who are grumpy most of the time, regardless of the circumstances, are likely to annoy other people.

The temperament of your students influences you. Teachers' evaluations of student abilities, level of adjustment, and intelligence are highly influenced by their perceptions of their temperament (Keogh, 2003). Teachers consistently view their students as more teachable if they regard their temperaments as easy.

Conclusion #6: Temperament classifies individuals. Recognizing the temperament of your students is facilitated by understanding how elementary students vary along a continuum of four dimensions (Lyons-Thomas & McClowry, 2012). Although temperament theorists vary in the labels that they attach to these dimensions,

---

BOX 1.2. AN FYI ABOUT SOME MISCONCEPTIONS ABOUT TEMPERAMENT

Now that you have begun to understand what temperament is, it's equally important to keep in mind what temperament is not. There are a number of common misconceptions about temperament that many people have. Temperament is not a synonym for "temper" or "temper tantrums." Although children with particular types of temperaments are more likely to have temper tantrums or to exhibit their negative reactions, temperament itself is a neutral concept. As a result, there are not good temperaments or bad temperaments. Temperament, instead, refers to normal variations in individuals and should never be equated with a behavioral disorder or psychiatric diagnosis.

Another misconception is that childhood temperament is the same as adult personality. Most temperament researchers regard temperament as the precursor or the core of personality (Teglasi, 2006). Although temperament continues to influence adult reactions, many people, as they get older, receive considerable feedback from their environment that causes them to adjust how they express their temperament. As a result, personality is more complex and incorporates thought processes, self-perceptions, defense mechanisms, values, and habits.

A final misperception is that you will lose control of your classroom if you respond to the individual needs of your students. Temperament-based classroom management does not mean that you accept student behavior that is disrespectful or disruptive. On the contrary, it emphasizes strategies that enhance classroom management and prevent or minimize such occurrences. In subsequent chapters, you will be presented with a number of temperament-based teacher strategies that have been shown to be effective in reducing student behavior problems and enhancing your confidence in handling them.

consensus is mounting that the following dimensions are relevant to school-age children (Mervielde & Asendorpf, 2000):

1. Motor activity
2. Task persistence
3. Withdrawal
4. Negative reactivity

In the following section, each of the dimensions will be defined. Then a synthesis will be presented of the many studies that have examined how these dimensions are related to other characteristics of children such as their gender, behavior, and academic outcomes.

MOTOR ACTIVITY

Motor activity refers to a student's tendency to move around and the propensity to be active. Some children have a high motor activity level no matter how the environment tries to restrain it. They are constantly in motion. For example, even when assigned seatwork, students who are high in motor activity will have difficulty sitting still. In contrast, students who are low in motor activity can sit quietly for long periods of time. Some may even need encouragement to be engaged in sports and other physical activities.

Motor Activity in the Classroom

Many studies have found that boys have higher motor activity levels than girls, although the effect size is not large (Else-Quest, Hyde, Goldsmith, & Van Hulle, 2006). Gender accounts for only 9 percent of the variance in motor activity (Lyons-Thomas & McClowry, 2012), which represents a small to medium effect size (Cohen, Cohen, West, & Aiken, 2003). The motor activity of children lessens as they get older (Lyons-Thomas & McClowry, 2012). Consequently, assessing the motor activity of children should take age into account. High motor is associated with externalizing behavior problems such as aggressive behavior (Guerin, Gottfried, Oliver, & Thomas, 2003) and lower academic achievement (Nelson, Martin, Hodge, Havill, & Kamphaus, 1999).

TASK PERSISTENCE

Task persistence is the student's tendency to stick with a task until it's done, even when interrupted. Students who are high in task persistence can complete their seatwork or other activities without being distracted. They also seem to derive satisfaction from engaging in work-related activities. Students who are low in task persistence, however, have difficulty working on class assignments or other projects without a concerted effort, not only on their part, but frequently their teachers' as well.

BOX 1.3. AN ILLUSTRATION OF MOTOR ACTIVITY IN THE CLASSROOM

Gregory: Can I go to the office to give the principal a note from my mom, Ms. Davis?

Ms. Davis: Not right now, Gregory. We're working on our art project. Please sit down so you can finish your work.

Ms. Davis: Gregory, will you please be careful? Otherwise, you're going to spill the paints.

—After a few short minutes—

Ms. Davis: Gregory, I told you that wiggling would cause a problem. You've spilled the paint all over the table. Go to the sink, get a rag, and wipe it up.

Task Persistence in the Classroom

During the preschool years, parental and teacher expectations of a child's ability to finish tasks are not very high. As soon as a child begins kindergarten, things rapidly change. Having a temperament that is high in task persistence is an advantage in school. Several studies of elementary school children show that the dimension of task persistence, compared to the three others, is the strongest predictor of adjustment and success at school (Guerin et al., 2003). High task persistence is associated with higher reading levels, better math achievement, and more social competence (Bramlett, Scott, & Rowell, 2000). In another study, children who had a lower IQ but

BOX 1.4. AN ILLUSTRATION OF TASK PERSISTENCE IN THE CLASSROOM

Ms. Jennings: Okay, kids, now that we've finished our lesson on the discovery of America, it's time for you to complete your workbook exercises. Answer the questions on pages 10 and 11.

Hilary: This won't take long. I already know the answers.

Ms. Jennings: I see that Hilary has already started on her workbook pages. Gregory, you seem to be having difficulty getting started. Please find your pencil and begin your worksheets.

—A few minutes later—

Hilary: That wasn't hard.

Ms. Jennings: Gregory? Please concentrate on your assignment. Some of the other children have already completed their work.

whose temperament was high in task persistence had better reading achievement than the students who had the same level of intelligence but were low in task persistence (Newman, Noel, Chen, & Matsopoulos, 1998).

Students with temperaments that are low in task persistence are disadvantaged in the majority of classrooms often because teachers find them difficult to teach (Keogh, 2003). Such children, however, are more affected by instructional method than their highly task-persistent peers (Schoen & Nagel, 1994). Strategies to enhance teacher effectiveness with students who are low in task persistence are presented in subsequent chapters of this book.

Gender also makes a difference, although not a large one. Consistently across studies, boys have lower levels of task persistence than their female classmates (Else-Quest et al., 2006). However, in a recent study based on teacher reports, gender accounted for only 5 percent of the difference (Lyons-Thomas & McClowry, 2012), which is a small effect size (Cohen et al., 2003). In other words, gender plays only a small role in explaining students' task persistence.

WITHDRAWAL

Withdrawal is a student's first reaction to new people or novel situations. Students who are high in withdrawal seem shy. They tend to withdraw when meeting people or when they encounter new situations. Students with temperaments that have the opposite tendency, however, are usually excited about meeting people or engaging in new experiences. In fact, they will often initiate such events.

Withdrawal in the Classroom

The temperament dimension of withdrawal influences student performance primarily through its impact on their social and emotional adjustment (Sanson, Hemphill, & Smart, 2004). High withdrawal manifests itself in a reticence to engage in social interactions when presented with novel situations (Martin, 1994). Students whose

---

BOX 1.5. AN ILLUSTRATION OF WITHDRAWAL IN THE CLASSROOM

Ms. Davis:	Good afternoon, Ms. Peters. You must be our new student, Coretta. Please come in, Coretta—and welcome to our classroom. The rest of the class is still at recess, but Freddy is waiting to meet you.
Freddy:	Hi! I'm Freddy. Want to see our hamster?
Coretta:	No.
Freddy:	How about our library corner?
Coretta:	I don't think so.
Freddy:	Okay. Would you like to see our new DVD about the pilgrims?
Coretta:	I guess so.

temperaments are high in withdrawal are less successful in relating to teachers and peers than their more social classmates who are low in withdrawal (Rudasill & Konold, 2008).

Students' tendency to withdraw when unfamiliar academic content is presented can compromise educational achievement (Birch & Ladd, 1998; Guerin et al., 2003). Unless the classroom environment is very responsive to a child who is high in withdrawal, school is likely to be perceived as increasingly stressful as time goes on (Martin & Holbrook, 1985).

Different from the other three dimensions of school-age temperament, there were no differences in withdrawal attributable to gender (Lyons-Thomas & McClowry, 2012). In other words, boys are just as likely as girls to be high or low in withdrawal.

NEGATIVE REACTIVITY

Negative reactivity is a student's tendency to have a negative reaction to life situations. A pupil who is high in negative reactivity will have an intense, immediate negative reaction to even a minor inconvenience. The student may exhibit high negative reactivity through facial expressions, body language, tone of voice, and/or verbal comments. Some people describe children who are high in negative reactivity as having "an attitude." In contrast, a student who is low in negative reactivity is generally pleasant and mild in his or her reactions to situational changes.

Negative Reactivity in the Classroom

Similar to task persistence, gender has only a small effect on negative reactivity in the classroom. Although teachers often perceive boys to be higher in negative reactivity than girls, gender accounts for only 3 percent of the difference (Lyons-Thomas &

BOX 1.6. AN ILLUSTRATION OF NEGATIVE REACTIVITY IN THE CLASSROOM

Ms. Davis: Children, I just got a call from Dr. Lewis, the paleontologist at the museum. He's sick and will not be at work this week.

Gregory: But we're supposed to go to the museum tomorrow. He was going to tell us how he discovered a new dinosaur. We never get to do anything fun!

Ms. Davis: I know that this is disappointing, Gregory.

Hilary: Can we go see the museum next week?

Ms. Davis: Dr. Lewis said that if we come next week, the museum will have a DVD ready that shows him on a dinosaur dig in Utah.

Hilary: Will we get to see it?

Ms. Davis: That's what he said.

Gregory: Who wants to see a dumb DVD anyway?

McClowry, 2012). A recent meta-analysis of many previous studies on child tempera-ment also found that gender is only minimally related to this dimension (Else-Quest et al., 2006).

Similar to the other three temperament dimensions, however, negative reactivity is neither good nor bad. Admittedly, students who are high in negative reactivity are often regarded as annoying or frustrating. Teachers may feel that no matter what they do, the child who is high in negative reactivity remains distressed. Moreover, children who are high in negative reactivity are not flexible. When upset, which happens fre-quently, they tend to "get stuck" and are not able to switch gears or to take in new information.

THEORETICAL FRAMEWORKS THAT SUPPORT TEMPERAMENT-BASED CLASSROOM MANAGEMENT

Classrooms are fast-paced environments with multiple interactions occurring simul-taneously among the students, and between teachers and their students. During the course of any school day, teachers make many rapid decisions based on the behavior of their students. Good and Brophy (2008) spent decades observing teachers in their classrooms. They found that teachers are more accurate observers when they have a method for labeling and analyzing classroom behavior. Applying conceptual labels brings teachers' reactions to a conscious level and facilitates their accuracy in report-ing their students' behaviors.

When observations are unified into an organized system with conceptual labels, it is called a theory. One advantage to using a theory to explain a behavioral phenom-enon is that it predicts patterns that are likely to occur. For example, a well-developed classroom management theory will explain and predict student behavior and, thereby, assist teachers in responding more effectively to their students and prevent disruptive behavior from occurring.

Temperament theory lends itself to supporting classroom management. Many teachers and practitioners in other fields, as well as parents, find understanding child temperament appealing because it systematically formalizes the behavioral response patterns they observe among children. A number of temperament frameworks have been elucidated that inform teachers how to use temperament-based strategies that are insightful, responsive, and effective.

The most frequently discussed theoretical framework for temperament-based intervention is the Goodness of Fit Model that was first introduced by Chess and Thomas, who are credited with being pioneers in the temperament field. Chess and Thomas (1984) maintained that a child's adjustment depends on whether there is goodness of fit, which is the match of the child's temperament to the demands, expec-tations, and opportunities of the environment. When goodness of fit occurs, positive development is anticipated. On the other hand, when there is a mismatch or "poor-ness of fit" between the child's temperament and the environment, behavior problems are likely to develop. To achieve goodness of fit, teachers and parents are encouraged to adjust the environment to the temperament of a child.

Sidebar 1.2. Temperament Pioneers: Chess and Thomas

When they began studying child temperament in 1956, Drs. Stella Chess and Alexander Thomas were recently married psychiatrists working in New York City. They began their New York Longitudinal Study (NYLS) in reaction to the prevailing behaviorism and psychoanalytic theories of that time. Both theories concluded that regardless of a child's adjustment problems, his or her mother was to blame. As practicing psychiatrists, parents of four children (two of whom were adopted), and as keen observers of the world, Chess and Thomas proposed a paradigm shift.

They began to explore how children contributed to their own development (Thomas, Chess, Birch, Hertzig, & Korn, 1963). Their NYLS, which included 138 primarily white, middle- to upper-class infants and their families, continued for more than thirty years (Chess & Thomas, 1990). They also studied child and parent-child interactions with low-income Puerto Rican families.

Chess and Thomas identified dimensions of child temperament and common typologies. More importantly, they explicated how interpersonal and environmental conditions led to children's adjustment or maladjustment. Initially, their research on children's temperament was deemed controversial because it deviated from the mainstream. Today, Chess and Thomas's goodness of fit model, their research findings, and the practical applications they espoused continue to influence the development field—especially among practitioners and educators who conduct temperament-based interventions (McClowry & Collins, 2012).

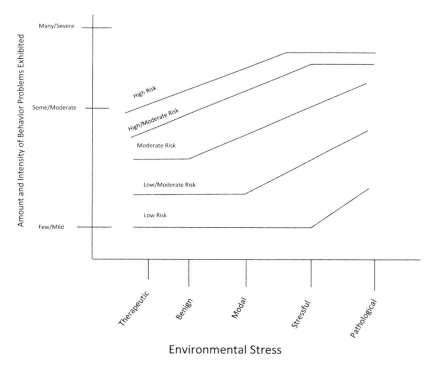

Figure 1.1 The Diathesis-Stress Model

The match/mismatch of children to their environmental contexts is further explicated by the Diathesis-Stress Model as applied to temperament theory by Martin (1994). As illustrated on the horizontal line in the above figure, home and school environments differ from therapeutic to pathological in the amount of stress they impose on children.

The vertical line refers to the predispositional risk that is attributed to a child's temperament. Children with challenging temperaments (those that most teachers and parents find difficult to manage) are at high risk for developing behavioral problems. Some environments, however, are therapeutic and are responsive and effective even for children with challenging temperaments. Consequently, children with challenging temperaments in therapeutic environments are likely to exhibit only moderate behavior problems. If, however, children with challenging temperaments are in stressful environments, they will probably develop more serious behavior problems.

In contrast, children with easy temperaments are generally at low risk for developing behavioral problems. Highly stressful or pathological environments, however, lack the personal, financial, and other resources to respond effectively to any children. In such environments, even children with easy temperaments will develop some behavior problems.

Both the Goodness of Fit and the Diathesis-Stress Models offer theoretical explanations on how children's temperament interacts with the environment. The results of many research studies support these models by demonstrating that children's adjustment is enhanced by parents and teachers who are responsive to children's temperaments (Rothbart & Bates, 2006). During middle childhood, a child's school and home are influential environments. Temperament-based classroom management aims to enhance the fit between a student's temperament and the classroom environment.

TEMPERAMENT-BASED CLASSROOM MANAGEMENT

Temperament-based classroom management is recognizing the temperament of students; creating a classroom community that is responsive to individual differences; and matching teacher management strategies to students' temperaments. Implementing temperament-based classroom management includes the **3 R**s followed by the **2 S**s: **R**ecognize child temperament, **R**eframe your perceptions, and **R**espond in ways that enhance environmental fit. Teachers then can **S**caffold their students when they encounter situations that are temperamentally challenging and gently apply strategies that **S**tretch a student's emotional, attentional, and/or behavioral repertoire.

INSIGHTS is a temperament-based classroom management program that has been tested in nearly two hundred classrooms. The efficacy of *INSIGHTS* was examined in three clinical trials funded by the United States' Institute of Education Sciences and National Institutes of Health. The results of a recent study demonstrated that *INSIGHTS*, compared to a control condition, enhances student engagement and teachers' practices in the classroom (Cappella et al., in press). In addition, the children in *INSIGHTS* gained in math and reading skills, sustained attention, and had fewer behavior problems (O'Connor, Cappella, McCormick, & McClowry, in press). Previous studies also showed that *INSIGHTS* reduces the behavior problems of children with attention deficit with hyperactivity disorder without the use of medications and increases the caregiving competency of their parents and teachers (McClowry, Snow, & Tamis-LeMonda, 2005; O'Connor, Rodriguez, Cappella, Morris, & McClowry, 2012). More information about *INSIGHTS* and a list of the peer-reviewed publications that describe its impact are available at www.insightsintervention.com and www.steinhardt.nyu.edu/insights.

SUMMARY

In this chapter, temperament is defined as the consistent reaction style that a child demonstrates across a variety of settings and situations, particularly those that involve stress or change. Temperament is biologically based and resistant to change. It also influences social interactions, predicts behavior, and modulates perceptions of experiences. The temperament of school-age children is classified on four dimensions. Motor activity is a student's tendency to be active. Task persistence is a student's propensity to complete a task even when interrupted. Withdrawal is a student's initial reaction to new people and situations. Negative reactivity refers to students' tendency to have a negative reaction to life situations.

Two models, Goodness of Fit and Diathesis-Stress, provide theoretical support for temperament-based interventions. Goodness of fit refers to the match between the environment and a child's temperament. Positive adjustment is anticipated when there is a good fit, and maladjustment can be expected if there is a poor fit. Diathesis-stress explains how children with easy temperaments are at lower risk for adjustment problems than those whose temperaments are challenging. Highly stressful environments, however, can compromise the development of children with easy temperaments and are especially harmful for children with challenging temperaments.

The central premise of temperament-based classroom management is that every student has inherent characteristics that have the potential to blossom if provided with a responsive classroom environment. Temperament-based classroom management recognizes the temperament of students, creates a classroom community that is responsive to individual differences, and applies teacher management strategies that match students' temperaments. Additional ways to recognize student temperaments are presented in the next chapter. The relationships between student temperaments and teacher perceptions are also explored. Then reframing is introduced as a strategy to enhance goodness of fit in the classroom.

CLASS DISCUSSION

- Hopefully, in your life you have been in environments that provided goodness of fit. In addition to feeling comfortable, you probably felt appreciated as a person and for your contributions. Discuss a situation in which you experienced goodness of fit. Then contrast it with a time when there was poorness of fit.
- Imagine under what circumstances a seven- or twelve-year-old student might experience poorness of fit with his or her classroom teacher. What kind of behavioral and emotional reactions are likely to occur? How will the child's temperament influence those behaviors?
- Imagine that you are ten years old. How do you think your teacher would describe your temperament on each of the four dimensions?

OPTIONAL CASE STUDY ASSIGNMENT

The theory on which temperament-based classroom management is based and the strategies derived from it are best learned in an experiential fashion. Beginning in this chapter and continuing throughout the book, assignments are suggested to help you apply the content of this book. The ideal way is to conduct case studies on two students. (Of course, tell the children's parents about your assignment and request their permission to engage with their child.)

If you do not have access to students, there are alternative ways to complete the assignments. If you are observing a classroom, engage the classroom teacher in completing the assignments with you. Another alternative is to apply the strategies you learn to two children in the community in which you live. They could be neighbors, nieces or nephews, or even your own children. At the end of the semester, compile the information you gathered into a portfolio. Be creative! This can be a fun assignment.

Case Study Assignment 1: Filling Out the Teacher School-Age Temperament Inventory

Begin by targeting two students. "Student E" should be one that you consider to be "easy." What are his or her initials? _____

Then, select another student who is "challenging" for you. Let's call him or her "Student C." What are his or her initials? _____

With Student E in mind, fill out the following questionnaire: http://insights intervention.com/tool/teachers/temperament-profile. After you answer the questions, a temperament profile will be automatically generated. Print out the profile so that you can refer to it as you progress though the book and work on your case study assignment. Then create a profile for Student C. (If you do not know the students well, ask their teacher to fill out the questionnaires for you.)

Case Study Assignment 2: Observation Guide for Students E and C

Observe your two targeted children when they have to deal with a change in the schedule or with another mildly stressful event. For example, one of your targeted students might want some class materials that another student is using. Or, what happens if an activity that the class has been looking forward to is postponed? Be sure to focus on the child's style of behavior in reaction to the event. Answer the following questions in one or two sentences and include the information in your portfolio:

1. What was the mildly stressful situation for Student E?
2. How did Student E react? Was it related to his or her temperament? If so, how?
3. What was the mildly stressful situation for Student C?
4. How did Student C react? Was it related to his or her temperament? If so, how?

RECOMMENDED READINGS

Keogh, B. K. (2003). *Temperament in the classroom: Understanding individual differences.* Baltimore, MD: Brookes.

McClowry, S., Snow, D. L., & Tamis-LeMonda, C. S. (2005). An evaluation of the effects of *INSIGHTS* on the behavior of inner city primary school children. *Journal of Primary Prevention, 26,* 567–584. doi:10.1007/s10935-005-0015-7

O'Connor, E. E., Cappella, E., McCormick, M. P., & McClowry, S. G. (in press). Enhancing the academic development of shy children: A test of the efficacy of *INSIGHTS. School Psychology Review.*

REFERENCES

Birch, S. H., & Ladd, G. W. (1998). Children's interpersonal behaviors and the teacher-child relationship. *Developmental Psychology, 34,* 934–946. doi:10.1037/0012-1649.34.5.934

Bramlett, R. K., Scott, P., & Rowell, R. K. (2000). A comparison of temperament and social skills in predicting academic performance in first graders. *Social Services in the Schools, 16*(1/2), 147–158. doi:10.1300/J008v16n01_10

Cappella, E., O'Connor, E. E., McCormick, M. P., Turbeville, A. E., Collins, A. (in press). Classwide efficacy of *INSIGHTS*: Observed student behaviors and teacher practices in kindergarten and first grade. *Elementary School Journal.*

Chess, S., & Thomas, A. (1984). *Origins and evolution of behavior disorders.* Cambridge, MA: Harvard University Press.

Chess, S., & Thomas, A. (1990). The New York Longitudinal Study: The young adult periods. *Canadian Journal of Psychiatry, 35*(6), 557–561.

Cohen, J., Cohen, P., West, S. G., & Aiken, L. S. (2003). *Applied multiple regression/correlation analysis for the behavioral sciences* (3rd ed.). Mahwah, NJ: Lawrence Erlbaum Associates.

Deary, I. J. (2000). Simple information processing and intelligence. In R. J. Sternberg (Ed.), *Handbook of intelligence* (pp. 267–284). New York, NY: Cambridge University Press.

Else-Quest, N. M., Hyde, J. S., Goldsmith, H. H., & Van Hulle, C. A. (2006). Gender differences in temperament: A meta-analysis. *Psychological Bulletin, 132*(1), 33–72. doi:10.1037/0033-2909.132.1.33

Good, T. L., & Brophy, J. E. (2008). *Looking in classrooms* (10th ed.). Boston, MA: Allyn and Bacon.

Guerin, D. W., Gottfried, A. W., Oliver, P. H., & Thomas, C. W. (2003). *Temperament: Infancy through adolescence.* New York, NY: Kluwer Academic.

Keogh, B. K. (2003). *Temperament in the classroom: Understanding individual differences.* Baltimore, MD: PH Brookes.

Lyons-Thomas, J., & McClowry, S. G. (2012). An examination of the construct validity and reliability of the Teacher School-Age Temperament Inventory. *Journal of Classroom Interaction, 47*(2), 25–32.

Martin, R. P. (1994). Child temperament and common problems in schooling: Hypotheses about causal connections. *Journal of School Psychology, 32*, 119–134. doi:10.1016/0022 -4405(94)90006-X

Martin, R. P., & Holbrook, J. (1985). Relationship of temperament characteristics to the academic achievement of first-grade children. *Journal of Psychoeducational Assessment, 3*, 131–140. doi:10.1177/073428298500300204

McClowry, S. G., & Collins, A. (2012). Temperament-based intervention: Reconceptualized from a response to intervention framework. In R. Shiner & M. Zentner (Eds.), *Handbook of childhood temperament* (pp. 607–627). New York, NY: Guilford Press.

McClowry, S. G., Snow, D. L., & Tamis-LeMonda, C. S. (2005). An evaluation of the effects of *INSIGHTS* on the behavior of inner city primary school children. *Journal of Primary Prevention, 26*, 567–584. doi:10.1007/s10935-005-0015-7

Mervielde, I., & Asendorpf, J. B. (2000). Variable-centered versus person-centered approaches to childhood personality. In S. E. Hampson (Ed.), *Advances in Personality Psychology* (pp. 37–76). Philadelphia, PA: Taylor & Francis.

Nelson, B., Martin, R. P., Hodge, S., Havill V., & Kamphaus, R. (1999). Modeling prediction of elementary school adjustment from preschool temperament. *Personality and Individual Differences, 26*, 687–700.

Newman, J., Noel, A., Chen, R., & Matsopoulos, A. S. (1998). Temperament, selected moderating variables, and early reading achievement. *Journal of School Psychology, 36*, 215–232.

O'Connor, E. E., Cappella, E., McCormick, M. P., & McClowry, S. G. (in press). Enhancing the academic development of shy children: A test of the efficacy of *INSIGHTS*. *School Psychology Review*.

O'Connor, E. E., Rodriguez, E. T., Cappella, E., Morris, J. G., & McClowry, S. G. (2012). Child disruptive behavior and parenting sense of competence: A comparison of the effects of two models of *INSIGHTS*. *Journal of Community Psychology, 40*, 555–572. doi:10.1002/jcop.21482

Rothbart, M., & Bates, J. (2006). Temperament. In W. Damon & R. Lerner (Eds.), *Handbook of Child Psychology: Vol. 3. Social, emotional, and personality development* (6th ed., pp. 99–166). New York, NY: Wiley.

Rudasill, K. M., & Konold, T. R. (2008). Contributions of children's temperament to teachers' judgments of social competence from kindergarten through second grade. *Early Education and Development, 19*(4), 643–666. doi:10.1080/10409280802231096

Sanson, A., Hemphill, S. A., & Smart, D. (2004). Connections between temperament and social development: A review. *Social Development, 13*(1), 142–170. doi:10.1046/j.1467-9507.2004.00261.x

Saudino, K. J. (2005). Behavioral genetics and child temperament. *Developmental and Behavioral Pediatrics, 26*(3), 214–223. doi:10.1097/00004703-200506000-00010

Schoen, M. J., & Nagel, R. J. (1994). Prediction of school readiness from kindergarten temperament scores. *Journal of School Psychology, 32*(2), 135–147. doi:10.1016/0022-4405(94)90007-8

Shiner, R. L., Buss, K. A., McClowry, S. G., Putman, S. P., Saudino, K. J., & Zentner, M. (2012). What is temperament now? Assessing progress in temperament research in the 25 years following Goldsmith et al. (1987). *Child Development Perspectives, 6*, 436–444. doi:10.1111/j.1750-8606.2012.00254.x

Strelau, J. (2008). *Temperament as a regulator of behavior: After fifty years of research*. Clinton Corners, NY: Eliot Werner.

Teglasi, H. (2006). Temperament. In G. G. Bear & K. M. Minke (Eds.), *Children's needs III: Development, prevention, and intervention* (pp. 391–403). Washington, DC: National Association of School Psychologists.

Thomas, A., Chess, S., Birch, H. G., Hertzig, M. E., & Korn, S. (1963). *Behavioral individuality in early childhood*. New York, NY: NYU Press.

CHAPTER 2

REFRAMING YOUR PERCEPTIONS

IMAGINE peering into a kaleidoscope. Gaze at the bright colors that are arranged in spectacular patterns. Picture making the slightest movement with your wrist and watch the images shift into another stunning view. Move your hand again and see how other shapes magically appear. Kaleidoscopes fascinate not only children, but many adults, too. Simple materials such as small pebbles, pieces of colored glass, and jewelry beads shift seamlessly into endlessly beautiful visual displays.

Temperament-based classroom management is like observing your classroom through a kaleidoscope. Suddenly you view the behavior and temperamental expressions of your students from a slightly different viewpoint. This chapter builds on the previous one by presenting additional teacher strategies that transform your day-to-day student observations into fascinating new perspectives about their temperament.

IN THIS CHAPTER:

- Four common temperament profiles are introduced.

- A comparison is made of the empirical and intuitive methods for recognizing the temperament of children.

- The repercussions of a student's salient temperament dimensions are explored.

- Teacher perceptions and attitudes toward their students' temperaments are discussed.

- Cautions about labeling children are offered.

- Reframing is offered as a teacher strategy critical for enhancing goodness of fit.

- Support is given for the supposition that temperament exists on a continuum.

COMMON TEMPERAMENT PROFILES OF SCHOOL-AGE CHILDREN

In the last chapter, the temperament of school-age children was introduced by describing four separate temperament dimensions. You were encouraged to observe your students to see whether they were high or low on each of the temperament dimensions. An alternative way to recognize the temperament of children is based on profiles that classify individuals into categorically different groups (Robins, John, Caspi, Moffitt, & Stouthamer-Lober, 1996). Temperament profiles are also called typologies.

You met four students in the last chapter: Hilary, Coretta, Freddy, and Gregory. Each of the students has a distinctive temperament with a different combination of temperament dimensions on which they are either high or low. The profiles of the students are empirically based and were first derived from data provided by 883 mothers of children ages four to twelve years who completed a questionnaire called the *School-Age Temperament Inventory* (SATI) (McClowry, 2002a).

More recent analyses closely replicated those results with data from two diverse groups of elementary school teachers who filled out a teacher version of the tool called the *Teacher School-Age Temperament Inventory* (T-SATI, pronounced "tee-say-tee") (Lyons-Thomas & McClowry, 2012; McClowry et al., 2013). The T-SATI is the questionnaire that you filled out when you answered questions about "Student E" and "Student C."

Patterns in the data from the parents and teachers identify four common temperament profiles of school-age children. Two profiles, *high maintenance* and *industrious*, involve three temperament dimensions: *negative reactivity*, *task persistence*, and *motor activity*. The other two profiles, *social/eager to try* and *cautious/slow to warm*, consist of only one dimension: *withdrawal*.

The statistics from the temperament profiles were transformed into graphics and multimedia teaching tools that are used in *INSIGHTS*. Videotaped vignettes teach the intervention content to teachers and to parents. Child actors depicting different temperaments convey how they react differently to daily life at school and at home. The vignettes also show how teachers and parents can use temperament-based strategies to enhance goodness of fit.

ICON 2.1

Goodness of fit occurs when the demands, expectations, and opportunities of the environment match an individual's temperament (Chess & Thomas, 1984).

The teachers resonate with the content presented in vignettes and further explicated in handouts and facilitated sessions as their comments support:

"I have been teaching for more than twenty years and sometimes I forget to implement strategies in my classroom. The program put me back in charge. Just like you say: not all strategies work for all students, but you have to continue to implement them to find out what works. If it does not, put those strategies to the side. You may need them next year."

"It was well worth the time. I'm not just aware that children have different temperaments, but adults also have different temperaments. By keeping this in mind, it helps me to respond in a more productive way."

The comments of parents also support that they find the content useful. One of the parents remarked,

"Little by little, I am getting along better with my son. We still have a lot of work to do with each other. The good part is that I know that I am in right direction."

To make the profiles age-appropriate for primary grade children, the data were morphed into four puppets who demonstrate how situations that are easy for one puppet (i.e., give a talk in front of the whole class) are challenging for another. The children are encouraged to expand their empathy skills as they get to know the different puppets with their respective temperaments. The puppets and the children also work together to resolve daily dilemmas that are shown in videotaped vignettes and those that occur in their daily lives. Storybooks depict other challenging situations that are best handled by employing empathy and dilemma-solving skills.

As anticipated, the children have been delighted to meet the puppets and to engage in activities with them. After the ten-week classroom program is completed, each student is asked: *Which puppet is most like you?* and *Which puppet would you like to be your best friend?* The comments of the children demonstrate how insightful primary grade children can be about temperament differences. Many children, even those in kindergarten, can identify their own temperament and that of their friends. In the following section, each of the profiles is presented along with some of the children's comments.

The four common school-age temperament profiles are called the Dynamic Four. They are *Freddy the Friendly*, who is social and eager to try; *Coretta the Cautious*, who is shy and slow to warm; *Hilary the Hard Worker*, who is industrious; and *Gregory the Grumpy*, whose temperament is high maintenance. Perhaps they remind you of children (or adults!) that you know. At least half of the students in an average classroom will be similar to one of the profiles. Other students will not match any of the typologies because they have a temperament that is high or low on a different combination of dimensions.

Freddy the Friendly has a temperament profile that is social and eager to try. His temperament is low in the withdrawal temperament dimension. Freddy is driven by his need to be with people and to try new experiences. Consequently, he is usually pleasant and has a zest for life that often draws others to him. Friends and family are

His temperament profile is:
Low in withdrawal

FREDDY THE FRIENDLY

NEGATIVE REACTIVITY	TASK PERSISTENCE	WITHDRAWAL	MOTOR ACTIVITY
HIGH	HIGH	HIGH	HIGH
		X	
LOW	LOW	LOW	LOW

Figure 2.1 Freddy the Friendly Is Social and Eager to Try

important to Freddy. He greets new experiences with enthusiasm because they provide additional opportunities to meet and be with people.

Freddy is usually excited about school because it provides opportunities to be with his friends. Freddy's teacher, however, worries about his safety. She is concerned because in Freddy's eagerness to try new things, he does not always demonstrate the best judgment. His teacher also thinks that he may be at risk for getting into trouble because he is so eager to try new experiences and make new friends.

When first and second graders in *INSIGHTS* were asked to select the puppet that is most like them, children who perceived themselves to be like Freddy made the following comments:

"Because I'm excited a lot. . . . If I go to school, I get excited. If I go home, I get excited. And if I'm going somewhere that I may think is boring, I still get excited."

"I'm really happy sometimes and sometimes I'm just a little too friendly."

The children who chose Freddy as their best friend did so because:

"He's friendly and nice to people."

"He likes to share his stuff."

Students who are social and eager to try initiate more interactions with their teachers than children with other types of temperaments (Rudasill & Rimm-Kaufman, 2009). Boys and girls are equally represented on this profile (McClowry et al., 2013).

Coretta the Cautious has a temperament profile that is shy and slow to warm. Because she is high in withdrawal, her first reaction is to avoid new situations and new people. With time and an appropriate amount of support, however, Coretta usually feels more comfortable and is able to be more responsive.

Her temperament profile is:
High in withdrawal

CORETTA THE CAUTIOUS

NEGATIVE REACTIVITY	TASK PERSISTENCE	WITHDRAWAL	MOTOR ACTIVITY
HIGH	HIGH	HIGH	HIGH
		X	
LOW	LOW	LOW	LOW

Figure 2.2 Coretta Is Cautious and Slow to Warm

The children in *INSIGHTS* who perceived themselves as being most like Coretta made the following observations:

"Every time I go in a new class, I get shy."

"I'm shy. Sometimes I don't want to be the line leader. I don't want to be first."

Many of the children in *INSIGHTS* were protective of Coretta, as evidenced by some of the comments of those who wanted her to be their best friend:

"Well, because we both sometimes are shy to meet new people and I'm shy to go to parties and learn new games and go on stage. I have stage fright."

"I can help her a lot and she can lighten up."

Children with temperaments that are cautious are perceived as unengaged at school (Rudasill & Konold, 2008). Likewise, their interactions with peers and adults are not assertive. Instead they are reticent to raise their hand and hesitate to participate in group projects. Compared to their more social students, teachers tend to be less aware of their cautious students and often underestimate their IQ (Martin & Holbrook, 1985). However, teachers view cautious students as more cooperative and compliant than other children. Parents report that 8 percent of children have temperaments that are cautious/slow to warm (McClowry, 2002a). Boys and girls in classrooms are equally represented on this profile (McClowry et al., 2013). Yet, teachers and parents react to girls and boys who are cautious differently. Adults are usually more tolerant of girls who are cautious than they are of boys (Rudasill & Konold, 2008).

INSIGHTS had a positive impact on the academic development of cautious children (O'Connor, Cappella, McCormick, & McClowry, in press). Compared to cautious children in a supplemental reading program that served as an attention control

Her temperament profile is:
Low in negative reactivity
High in task persistence
Low in activity

HILARY THE HARD WORKER

NEGATIVE REACTIVITY	TASK PERSISTENCE	WITHDRAWAL	MOTOR ACTIVITY
HIGH	HIGH	HIGH	HIGH
	X		
X			X
LOW	LOW	LOW	LOW

Figure 2.3 Hilary the Hard Worker Is Industrious

group, the shy children in *INSIGHTS* showed greater growth in math skills and in critical thinking. They also demonstrated increases in classroom engagement compared to their classmates who were not shy.

Hilary the Hard Worker has a temperament profile that is industrious. Because she is high in task persistence and low in activity, she can sit for long periods of time while independently doing seatwork or when working on a class project. School is important to Hilary. She takes great pride in her work and likes to please her teacher. Still, Hilary has been known to be upset when she does not have enough time to finish an activity that she has started or when her assignment is not completed to her level of satisfaction. Hilary tends to be a perfectionist.

When there are changes in plans Hilary usually handles the disappointment well because she is low in negative reactivity. Her teacher, however, is concerned that Hilary is not assertive enough in getting her own needs met because she is low in negative reactivity. The children in *INSIGHTS* who viewed themselves as Hilary the Hard Worker made the following statements:

"I'm a hard worker. I can do my work without running around."

"I do all my work, sit down, and listen to the teacher. I can finish my work easily."

Children who chose Hilary as their best friend did so for the following reasons:

"We both like to work hard and we both like to draw and we both like to experience things and learn a lot of things."

"She's a hard worker. If she was in my class and I didn't know how to do my work, she could help me."

Children with industrious temperaments are advantaged in the vast majority of classrooms where the expectation is that students sit quietly and listen attentively

His temperament profile is:
High in negative reactivity
Low in task persistence
High in activity

GREGORY THE GRUMPY

NEGATIVE REACTIVITY	TASK PERSISTENCE	WITHDRAWAL	MOTOR ACTIVITY
HIGH	HIGH	HIGH	HIGH
X			X
	X		
LOW	LOW	LOW	LOW

Figure 2.4 Gregory the Grumpy Is High Maintenance

for an extended amount of time. Consequently, it is no surprise that industrious students are perceived as being highly teachable and as socially competent by their teachers (Keogh, 1994). About 10 percent of children have industrious temperaments (McClowry, 2002a). Girls are disproportionately represented in profiles characterized by an industrious temperament. Teachers report that twice as many girls have an industrious temperament compared to boys (McClowry et al., 2013).

Gregory the Grumpy has a temperament profile that is high maintenance. He reacts strongly and negatively to changes or stress because his temperament is high in negative reactivity. Gregory gets upset easily and can be very moody. Some people say he has an "attitude." His dad prefers to think of Gregory as just being honest.

Gregory often has problems finishing seatwork or completing his homework because he is low in task persistence. Gregory is also high in activity. Consequently, he has difficulty sitting still. He wiggles constantly. On the positive side, Gregory can be a leader because he is comfortable making decisions and expressing his opinions even when others disagree.

The children in *INSIGHTS* who viewed themselves as being like Gregory gave the following explanations:

"I walk around the class a lot and I don't do my homework."

"Sometimes it's hard to do stuff like concentrate on my work and I get mad."

A small number of the children selected Gregory as a best friend because they recognized their own reactions as similar to his:

"Sometimes I can be grumpy like him."

Another child said:

"I'm like Gregory. He complains too much, which is funny."

Other children expressed empathy for Gregory as the following quote implies:

"Sometimes he's friendly and he needs a friend."

These comments from young children help adults understand that children whose temperament is like Gregory's often have interactions with others that can be uncomfortable or frustrating for both parties. If you have a student whose temperament profile is like Gregory's (and it is highly likely that you will), understand that being high maintenance is not easy. Children with a high maintenance temperament expend a great deal of energy trying to complete their assignments or engaging in interactions that they find onerous (Strelau, 2008). Likewise, the "Gregorys" perceive minor situations as difficult to handle and are easily distressed by them. Children with a high maintenance temperament are often aware that their peers and the adults in their life find their behavior annoying. Even though the puppet version of Gregory in *INSIGHTS* is a sensitive sort of grumpy person, the children sometimes describe him as "mean."

School can be frustrating for children with high maintenance temperaments. Students with this temperament profile are more likely to exhibit disruptive classroom behavior (Rothbart & Bates, 2006). They often have more difficulty in performing successfully at school including learning how to read.

Teachers are often frustrated with students who have a high maintenance temperament (Keogh, 2003; McClowry et al., 2010). The combination of high negative reactivity and motor activity and low persistence requires a great deal of teacher attention. Teachers initiate more interactions with their students with high maintenance temperaments compared to other children in their classrooms (Rudasill & Rimm-Kaufman, 2009). Although children with high maintenance temperaments can be challenging, effective teachers can make a real difference in their academic achievement. Such students are particularly affected by instruction method (Orth & Martin, 1994).

About 14 percent of children have temperaments that are high maintenance (McClowry, 2002a). Teachers report that twice as many boys compared to girls have a high maintenance temperament (McClowry et al., 2013). The disproportionate number of boys versus girls who are represented on the high maintenance temperament profile deserves serious examination because it has implications for classroom management. Many studies have concluded that boys are more disruptive than girls in classrooms (Rescorla et al., 2007). A more complex picture emerges when gender and temperament are examined simultaneously in relation to classroom behavior, as we found in a recent analysis (McClowry et al., 2013). Based on classroom observations and teacher reports, boys are indeed more disruptive than girls. However, when temperament is taken into account, the effect of gender on student disruptive behavior is not significant. Although there are fewer girls than boys who have high maintenance temperaments, teachers regard the girls as just as difficult to manage as the boys (McClowry et al., 2010). In other words, Gretchen the Grumpy is as challenging a student as Gregory the Grumpy!

INSIGHTS also had a positive impact on the academic and social behavior of children with high maintenance temperaments (McCormick, O'Connor, Cappella, & McClowry, 2014). Compared to children with the same temperaments in a supplemental reading program that served as an attention control group, the children with high maintenance temperaments demonstrated fewer behavior problems, were more academically engaged, and had less off-task behavior. The effects of the *INSIGHTS* program were partially attributable to an improved student/teacher relationship.

The Dynamic Four provide striking evidence that children differ in their temperament in substantial ways. Some children have easy temperaments that are a combination of two of the profiles (McClowry, 2002a). About 4 percent of children are both industrious like Hilary the Hard Worker and social/eager to try like Freddy the Friendly. Another 6 percent had temperaments that are very challenging because they are high maintenance like Gregory the Grumpy and cautious/slow to warm like Coretta. Of course, some children have temperaments that do not match any of the four common temperament profiles. Instead they exhibit a different combination of temperament dimensions. For example, a student might be low in task persistence and motor activity or might be high in task persistence and negative reactivity. Even if a particular student does not match any of the common profiles, comparing the student to the profiles helps to clarify how the child differs from his peers.

Another point to remember is that although the temperament profiles have names that indicate that they are male or female, they could be represented by either gender. The profiles could have just as easily been named Felicity the Friendly, Carl the Cautious, Henry the Hard Worker, and Gretchen the Grumpy, as figure 2.5 illustrates.

TWO METHODS FOR RECOGNIZING THE TEMPERAMENT OF STUDENTS

There are two methods you can use to recognize the temperaments of school-age children: *intuitive* or *empirical*. The difference between these two methods is comparable to relying on your general impressions of your students' math abilities or giving the

Figure 2.5 Carl the Cautious, Gretchen the Grumpy, Felicity the Friendly, and Henry the Hard Worker

children a math test to evaluate their skill levels. As will be discussed, both methods have advantages and disadvantages.

To use the intuitive method to recognize the temperament of students, pay close attention to the exemplars of the Dynamic Four as described in this book or as shown on the website http://www.insightsintervention.com/video/at-school/meet -the-kids-at-school.

Another way to recognize the temperaments of students is using the empirical method. As you did in the previous chapter, you can answer the thirty-three items on the *Teacher School-Age Temperament Inventory* (T-SATI; Lyons-Thomas & McClowry, 2012). When the temperament profile is generated, note whether a student was high, low, or intermediate on each of the four dimensions of school-age temperament: negative reactivity, task persistence, withdrawal, and motor activity. For example, the profile shown in figure 2.6 illustrates the temperament of a student by the name of Jodi. To interpret her temperament profile, begin by noting the four Xs. The empirical method demonstrates that Jodi is high in negative reactivity, low in task persistence, and high in motor activity. Jodi's score on withdrawal is in the intermediate range.

The scoring levels, as shown in figure 2.7, are derived from data acquired from a national sample of children who were students in regular elementary education classrooms (Lyons-Thomas & McClowry, 2012). Based on the Xs on the generated profiles, describe the temperament of the target students you have selected and answer the following questions: *What does the empirical method tell you about Student E? What does the empirical method tell you about Student C?*

Sometimes, teachers will find that their intuition does not match the ones derived from the empirical method. One of the reasons that discrepancies occur between the

NEGATIVE REACTIVITY	TASK PERSISTENCE	WITHDRAWAL	MOTOR ACTIVITY
HIGH	HIGH	HIGH	HIGH
X			X
3.0	4.0	3.1	2.80
		X	
2.1	2.9	2.3	1.8
	X		
LOW	LOW	LOW	LOW

Figure 2.6 Jodi's Temperament Profile

two methods is related to the flurry of interactions that occur simultaneously in a classroom. Due to the amount of observational stimuli teachers encounter, some student behaviors and circumstances become more memorable than others. Isolated dramatic incidents are likely to carry more weight when reporting on children's behavior than repeated nonevents or circumstances of low intensity (Gilovich, Griffin, & Kahneman, 2002). One advantage to the empirical method is that it reduces the biases inherent when reporting on one's perception by prompting a teacher to reflect on a broad range of situations posed by the questions. In other words, systematic observations replace overall impressions.

SALIENT TEMPERAMENT DIMENSIONS

Regardless of whether you are using the empirical method, or your intuition, or a combination of both, pay careful attention to those dimensions on which your student scored high or low (the gray or black boxes). Xs in the gray and black boxes are considered a student's *salient* dimensions. Students tend to be more consistent across settings and situations in relation to their salient temperament dimensions. Teachers often report that children whose salient temperament dimensions are in the black boxes (high negative reactivity, low task persistence, high withdrawal, and high activity) exhibit more *challenging* behaviors than those in the gray or white boxes. Conversely, teachers regard students as easy when their salient temperament dimensions are in the gray boxes. This generality, however, needs to be tempered with a reminder that no temperament is ideal in every situation, as we will discuss later in this chapter. Likewise, because teachers differ in the attributes that they value or find annoying, they may apply the *easy* or *challenging* descriptors to different temperaments.

Students who score in the intermediate range, which is the middle row of white boxes on figure 2.7, do not react consistently in relation to that dimension. For example, a child who scores in the center white box for task persistence may be persistent in some situations but not in others. The student may easily attend to a particular subject or assignment he or she likes. The same student may lack task persistence if an assignment involves something that the student perceives as "boring." The inconsistency in behaviors related to that dimension means that it is not a salient part of a student's temperament, but is likely to differ based on the child's motivation or environmental circumstances.

All but 2 percent of students are high or low on at least one dimension of temperament (Lyons-Thomas & McClowry, 2012). Rarely a child will, based on the empirical method, score in the middle of all four dimensions. Does that mean that the child does not have a temperament? No, but it does mean that the child has a mild temperament and, unless his or her teacher makes a concerted effort, the child may not receive as much attention as other students in the classroom. If you have a student who is in the intermediate range on all four dimensions, you will need to be especially attentive to be sure that the student does not get missed among his or her more "noticeable" classmates.

BOX 2.1. AN FYI ON THE STANDARDIZATION OF THE T-SATI

Lyons-Thomas and McClowry (2012) conducted a study to examine the psychometric properties of the *Teacher School-Age Temperament Inventory* (T-SATI), an adaptation of the *School-Age Temperament Inventory* (SATI), which is a parent report (McClowry, 1995). The data for the T-SATI was reported on an Internet site by 143 teachers from 27 states.

The teachers answered the questionnaire twice based on a randomly selected boy and girl from their classrooms. The students included 261 students in regular elementary school classrooms. The children came from a variety of communities with schools that varied greatly in the number of students that were eligible for free and reduced lunch. Approximately half of the students were Caucasian. The majority of the teachers were Caucasian women who were thirty-five years old or younger. Forty percent had taught five years or less.

A series of principal components analysis with varimax rotation were conducted to examine construct validity of the T-SATI. This type of analysis identifies how the questions group together into factors or dimensions. The questionnaire items were retained when they had a factor loading that was >.50 on one factor and had a .20 spread on the others. The results supported the same dimensions as found by McClowry (1995) on the parent report: negative reactivity, task persistence, withdrawal, and motor activity. Cronbach's alphas, which are a measure of internal reliability, were .90 to .96. Alphas that are greater than .80 are considered adequate reliability (Nunnally & Bernstein, 1994). Figure 2.7 shows the cutoff levels for each of the dimensions.

NEGATIVE REACTIVITY	TASK PERSISTENCE	WITHDRAWAL	MOTOR ACTIVITY
HIGH	HIGH	HIGH	HIGH
3.0	4.0	3.1	2.80
2.1	2.9	2.3	1.8
LOW	LOW	LOW	LOW

Figure 2.7 High, Intermediate, and Low Scores on the T-SATI

More information about the standardization of the T-SATI can be found at:
Lyons-Thomas, J., & McClowry, S. G. (2012). An examination of the construct validity and reliability of the Teacher School-Age Temperament Inventory. *Journal of Classroom Interaction, 47*(2), 25–32.

A FEW CAUTIONS ABOUT LABELING

The temperament profiles, in their various forms, have been presented to a variety of audiences: young children, teachers, parents, school and other community mental health professionals, and other academics. Whether represented by graphics, puppets, actors, or just written descriptions, the profiles resonate deeply with many people. Not only children, but many adults, recognize themselves as one of the Dynamic Four. Children and adults often gravitate toward the profile that is most like them.

Participants in the *INSIGHTS* program often comment that one or more of the profiles remind them of other people in their lives. You may be finding that this phenomenon is happening to you as well. Suddenly, you recognize the temperament of other people in your professional or personal lives.

Caution, however, must be expressed about telling someone, especially a student, that he or she is similar to one of the profiles. As demonstrated by the comments of the primary grade students in *INSIGHTS*, even young children can identify their own temperament. Self-identification, however, is different than being labeled by another person. Particularly if the profile has characteristics that you may not value, the person may feel misunderstood or unappreciated. For example, saying "You are a Gregory the Grumpy" is likely to be hurtful, especially if said in anger.

An important distinction needs to be made between recognizing an individual's temperament versus using it as a label. The temperament profiles presented in this book and on the website are intended to be reference points from which teachers, parents, and other school personnel can identify students and then strive to enhance goodness of fit for them.

TEACHER PERCEPTIONS AND ATTITUDES REGARDING STUDENT TEMPERAMENT

A number of studies have examined how teachers' perceptions and attitudes of teachers about the temperaments of their students influence a number of classroom-related variables. To interpret the results of these studies, a brief explanation on correlations is necessary. Correlations measure the strength or association of two variables with each other. They range from -1 to 1 (Cohen, 1988).

Correlations that are positive indicate that as the value of one of the variables goes up, so does the other. For example, studying for college tests is associated with a higher grade point. On the other hand, a negative correlation shows the opposite relationship. For example, high calorie consumption is negatively associated with weight loss. The strength of the association between variables is related to the absolute value of the correlations (Cohen, 1988). In general terms, 0 means there is no relationship, .10 is a small correlation, .30 is medium, and .50 and above are large, regardless of whether they are positive or negative.

Consider the differences in the strength of the correlations between teachers' perception of students' temperaments and IQ, academic achievement, and grades. Think about the implications of these associations between the temperaments of school-age children and IQ, standardized tests, and teacher-assigned grades.

Summary of correlations between student temperament and indexes of children's cognitive assessment

	Correlations	References
IQ	Small to medium	Guerin, Gottfried, Oliver, & Thomas, 2003; Keogh, 2003; Martin, Olejnik, & Gaddis, 1994
Standardized tests	Medium	Guerin et al., 2003; Martin & Holbrook, 1985
Teacher assigned grades	Medium to large	Guerin et al., 2003; Martin, 1988; Martin & Holbrook, 1985; Keogh, 2003

Not surprisingly, teacher perceptions of student temperament are more highly associated with grades than with standardized tests or IQ. A number of other factors are also likely to contribute to the differences between the strength of these correlations. Although intelligence varies substantially among children with all kinds of temperaments, students whose temperaments are high in task persistence and low in motor activity are advantaged when taking standardized tests. Among regular education students, these same temperament dimensions have a stronger association with reading achievement, and to a lesser extent math, than does intelligence (Guerin et al., 2003; Martin et al., 1994).

The decisions that teachers make regarding classroom discipline and referrals to special education and other services are particularly influenced by student task persistence and motor activity (Keogh, 2003). Teachers consider students more teachable if their temperament is high in task persistence, and low in activity, negative reactivity, and withdrawal (Keogh, 2003). Such students also are more likely to complete their assignments and homework and to respond in socially competent ways at school. These are the same temperament dimensions that were referred to as *easy* earlier in this chapter.

The practical implications of these associations between temperament and grades can be interpreted by returning to our kaleidoscope metaphor. Let's reexamine what goes on in the majority of elementary school classrooms through a temperament lens. Most teachers chose the profession because they wanted to teach. Yet, less than 10 percent of the students have industrious temperaments consisting of the dimensions regarded by teachers as ideal. Classrooms, however, consist of students with a variety of temperaments. Only a small percentage of students match the behavioral expectations of many teachers. Goodness of fit cannot occur if a teacher maintains that all students could be industrious, if only they tried harder. Instead temperament theory clarifies that the malleability of a child's behavior is limited by their temperament.

This chapter has presented you with a number of kaleidoscope experiences regarding the identification of the temperament of students. Temperament-based classroom management, however, has many more facets than just knowing the various dimensions or typologies. Once teachers learn how to recognize the temperaments of their students, they can advance to the next step, which is to reframe their perceptions. In the following scenario, notice how the two teachers have very different perceptions of the Dynamic Four.

REFRAMING YOUR PERCEPTIONS

A careful read of the scenario in box 2.2 demonstrates that although Lisa and Cathy were in agreement regarding the dimensions of temperament they recognized in their students, they differed dramatically in the meaning they attributed to their observations. Cathy's perspective was that an industrious temperament was ideal. Students with other types of temperament frustrated or annoyed her. Lisa had a different viewpoint: no temperament is ideal in every circumstance. All temperaments have strengths and possible concerns. Lisa was able to reframe her perspective in order to incorporate both a student's temperament strengths and possible concerns.

Reframing is changing one's viewpoint about a situation so that the "facts" are reinterpreted into a different perspective that is as good, or even better, than the original one (Nardone & Watzlawick, 1993; Watzlawick, Weakland, & Fisch, 1974). Although the circumstances remain the same, reframing softens an individual's logic and encourages reinterpretation. When reframing occurs, the meaning of a situation changes. So does the person with the new viewpoint. Once reframing occurs, an individual cannot return to the original perspective. Instead the individual has acquired a greater sensitivity to the nuances of the situation and has gained new insights into

---

BOX 2.2. IMAGINE THIS SCENE IN THE FACULTY LOUNGE

Lisa: Hi, Cathy. How has your first month been with my former students? The kids look so much taller when I see them in the hallways.

Cathy: Well, quite frankly, it hasn't been easy! Freddy appears to be more interested in talking to his friends than in learning what I'm teaching. And I'm worried about Coretta. She doesn't seem to be engaged. All the other kids are eager to answer my questions, but she remains quiet—even when I call on her. And then there's Gregory, who spends much, too much, time complaining and not enough time concentrating.

Lisa: Wow! Isn't that interesting! We have very different impressions about the same kids. I found that Freddy's enthusiasm about everything and everyone really energized the class. And Coretta started out quiet, but she talked a lot more as the year went on. Now, Gregory sure can be challenging, but I always enjoyed hearing his different perspective on life. What do you think accounts for the differences in our perspectives?

Cathy: I don't know, but I'm sure that we agree about Hilary. I wish the others were working as hard as she is.

Lisa: Actually, I was concerned about Hilary. She's such a perfectionist that she gets more distressed over her assignments than is necessary.

their meaning. Further reflection assists the reframer to select a different response based on the newly acquired perspective.

Reframing is a powerful temperament-based strategy when used to enhance goodness of fit. It allows teachers to appreciate the strength of their students while simultaneously acknowledging their temperament-related concerns. Table 2.1 lists those strengths and concerns in relation to high and low levels on each of the four temperament dimensions.

VIEWING TEMPERAMENT AS A CONTINUUM

A continuing controversy in the temperament field centers on the distinctions between child psychiatric disorders and temperament extremes. One position in the debate asserts that definitive child psychiatric problems can be reliably diagnosed with criteria from the *Diagnostic and Statistical Manual of Mental Disorders V* (American Psychiatric Association, 2013). Among the diagnoses applied to children are depression, anxiety, oppositional defiant disorder, and attention deficit with hyperactivity disorders. Taking a different perspective, noted scientists/practitioners Jensen, Knapp, and Mrazek (2006) assert that clear boundaries between normal mental health and psychopathology do not exist, especially for children. Instead cutoffs differ based on definition and clinical judgment. They also maintain that the majority of adjustment symptoms children exhibit result from adverse experiences or a mismatch between the child's needs and the environment's resources—in other words, poorness of fit.

Jensen and colleagues (2006) acknowledge that although DSM diagnoses are necessary for insurance and other types of reimbursement, they do not direct treatment in school settings. Instead children, with an assortment of diagnoses, are treated for the cluster of symptoms that compromise their ability to adequately function in the school environment. Often these symptoms overlap even when the official diagnoses are different.

Many children with adjustment problems exhibit both internalizing (such as anxiety or depression) and externalizing symptoms like oppositional behavior (McConaughy & Achenbach, 1994). Regardless, the treatment of children, both in schools and community mental health centers, is based on symptoms and geared toward improving the functionality and social competence of a child.

The other position in the debate on the distinction between temperament and child psychiatric disorders maintains that temperament exists on a continuum with a wide range of variations. A continuum is a sequence of elements that vary. For example, no score on a continuum is dramatically different from the scores near it. The extremes, however, are very different. For example, imagine lining up students at an elementary school according to their height. The differences between two children standing next to each other may be minimal and difficult to see. The height of the shortest child and the tallest, however, will be very different from each other.

From a temperament perspective, children at the extremes of temperament are at risk for developing a number of psychological symptoms (Rothbart & Bates, 2006). "At-risk" means more likely but not guaranteed. In a number of studies, children whose temperament was high in withdrawal were *at-risk* for having internalizing

Table 2.1. Temperament Strengths and Possible Concerns

Temperamental tendency		Strengths	Possible problems or teaching concerns
Task Persistence	High task persistence	Usually completes assignments or responsibilities without a lot of reminders.	May be difficult to get the child to stop once he or she begins something.
	Low task persistence	Is willing to switch from one activity to another easily. May be very creative.	Needs supervision to complete homework or other tasks.
Withdrawal	High withdrawal	Doesn't rush into situations.	Shy or even unwilling to try new activities or meet new people.
	High approach	Social; willing to try new things.	May be willing to take too many risks. Safety concerns about talking to strangers or trying something risky.
Activity	High activity	Energetic	Difficulty sitting still.
	Low activity	Quiet	May not engage in enough physical activities or sports.
Negative Reactivity	High negative reactivity	Honest about his or her feelings and opinions.	Complains frequently.
	Low negative reactivity	Easy to get along with.	May not be assertive.

behavior problems such as depression or anxiety (Guerin et al., 2003; Rothbart & Bates, 2006). Children with high maintenance temperaments were *at-risk* for exhibiting externalizing behaviors such as aggression and attentional difficulties (Guerin et al., 2003; McClowry et al., 2010).

The controversy between child psychiatric disorders and temperament extremes is particularly spirited regarding the diagnosis of attention deficit with hyperactivity disorder (ADHD). From a temperament perspective, the high maintenance temperament profile is similar to the symptoms attributed to ADHD. Empirical evidence supports this premise. Foley, McClowry, and Castellanos (2008) compared children whose parents brought them to a developmental neurology clinic for an evaluation of ADHD with other children who were seen in a pediatric clinic for well-child visits. The mothers at both clinics were interviewed with the ADHD module on the Diagnostic Interview for Children (Shaffer, Fisher, Lucas, Dulcan, & Schwab-Stone, 2000) and filled out a number of temperament and ADHD questionnaires. Large correlations (most in the range of .60–.90) were found between the ADHD questionnaires and task persistence, motor activity, and negative reactivity. Sixty-six percent of the children who received a diagnosis of ADHD had high maintenance temperaments—a percentage significantly higher than the 14 percent of children McClowry (2002a) reported among school-age children.

Not all children who have high maintenance temperaments or who are high in withdrawal have psychiatric problems. As discussed in the last chapter, goodness of fit makes a major difference in the mental health of children with challenging temperaments. Certainly, teachers and parents regard children with extreme temperaments as more arduous to manage (Foley et al., 2008). Reframing, however, can assist caregivers to view these children in a more responsive way. For example, the ADHD symptoms of inattentiveness, hyperactivity, and impulsivity can be reframed from an evolutionary, adaptational perspective (Jensen et al., 2006). Individuals with such characteristics were advantaged in our ancestral hunter-gatherer society. The ability to identify new opportunities, move quickly, and be vigilant for danger often meant survival not only for the individual and for others in the community who benefited from having a "response-ready" member.

The same attributes, however, can lead to poorness of fit in many contemporary school environments. Jensen and colleagues (2006) assert that today's classrooms often "demand attentional focus and motoric passivity while presenting complex stimuli. They offer many distractions (e.g., large class size), yet funnel information through one modality only, such as in passive listening or reading. They also limit opportunities for shifting attention and for motor response and demand delay of recognition for efforts" (p. 101). In the following chapters, strategies for enhancing goodness of fit for all students, including those whose temperament are at the extremes, will be offered.

SUMMARY

In this chapter, a kaleidoscope metaphor is used to illustrate how different strategies can help teachers identify the temperaments of students. Four common student temperament profiles are presented: *Freddy the Friendly* is social and eager to try with a temperament that is low in withdrawal. *Coretta the Cautious*'s temperament is the opposite of Freddy's. She is shy, slow to warm, and high in withdrawal. *Hilary the Hard Worker* is industrious and is high in task persistence and low in negative reactivity and motor activity. *Gregory the Grumpy* is high maintenance and has a temperament that is the opposite of Hilary's. He is low in task persistence and high in negative reactivity and motor activity.

Students' temperament profiles can be recognized intuitively or can be generated empirically by completing a questionnaire called the *Teacher School-Age Temperament*

Inventory. Both methods identify a student's salient temperament dimensions, which are the ones on which a child is high or low compared to other students. Teachers are encouraged to reframe their perceptions of their students' temperaments by understanding that each salient temperament dimension has strengths and possible areas of concern. Regardless of a student's temperament, it is important not to label a child with a particular temperament. Instead temperament profiles are used as a reference point among teachers, parents, and other school personnel. The temperament profiles also help teachers identify their own attitudes regarding students with various temperaments and are useful when accessing and enhancing goodness of fit.

Although some practitioners regard child psychiatric diagnoses as extremes of temperament, others think that temperament exists on a continuum without clear distinctions between mental health symptoms and psychopathology. The position of this book is that although children with challenging temperaments are at higher risk for behavioral disorders, children's adjustment always needs to be evaluated within an environmental context. Evaluating whether goodness of fit has been achieved at home and at school is essential to understanding a child's behavior problems.

In the next chapter, goodness of fit is elaborated upon in relation to teacher/student relationships. Responsive teachers are a positive influence on students' behavior and academic achievement. Strategies for enhancing teacher relationships with their students are presented.

CLASS DISCUSSION

- Identify characters in children's books, on television, or in movies that have temperaments like the ones described in this chapter. Discuss how the characters are similar or how they are different.

Figure 2.8
Graphics
for Popsicle
Stick Puppets

- Cut out the graphics of the four temperament profiles that are included at the end of this chapter in figure 2.8. Or download color versions of the graphics from the website at http://www.insightsintervention.com. Then attach the graphics to Popsicle sticks and use them to dramatize how children with each of the temperaments would react to one or more of the following scenarios:
  - Report cards are coming! Report cards are coming!
  - The field trip that the children have been waiting for is canceled due to severe weather conditions.
  - You're sick and there's a substitute teacher in your classroom.
  - A new student is assigned to your classroom.
  - A scenario derived from your own experiences.
- Check out these sites for virtual kaleidoscope experiences:
    http://inoyan.narod.ru/kaleidoskop.swf
    http://www.zefrank.com/dtoy_vs_byokal/
    http://minimalexposition.blogspot.com/2011/03/interactive-virtual-kaleido scope.html
- Recall the two teachers in the faculty lounge in box 2.2. Each had a different perspective about the same students. Role-play a faculty lounge discussion regarding students you have observed.

OPTIONAL CASE STUDY ASSIGNMENT

Observe Student E and Student C again. Based on what you know about your targeted students, select the salient temperament dimensions in table 2.1 that apply to your Student E and Student C. Then notice what strengths accompany those dimensions in column B. Related problems and teacher concerns that match your students' salient temperament dimensions are listed in column C. Consider the following questions:

1. What was the situation with Student E?
2. What salient temperament dimension(s) did Student E demonstrate?
3. What strengths did Student E demonstrate?
4. What problems or concerns are related to Student E's temperament as described in question 2?
5. What was the situation with Student C?
6. What salient temperament dimension(s) did Student C demonstrate?
7. What strengths did Student C demonstrate?
8. What problems or concerns are related to Student C's temperament as described in question 2?

RECOMMENDED READINGS

Foley, M., McClowry, S. G., & Castellanos, F. X. (2008). The relationship between attention deficit hyperactivity disorder and child temperament. *Journal of Applied Developmental Psychology, 29,* 157–169. doi:10.1016%2Fj.appdev.2007.12.005

McClowry, S. G. (2002a). The temperament profiles of school-age children. *Journal of Pediatric Nursing, 17*, 3–10. doi:10.1053%2Fjpdn.2002.30929

McClowry, S. G. (2002b). Transforming temperament profile statistics into puppets and other visual media. *Journal of Pediatric Nursing, 17*, 11–17. doi:10.1053%2Fjpdn.2002.30933

REFERENCES

American Psychiatric Association. (2013). *Diagnostic and statistical manual of mental disorders* (5th ed.). Arlington, VA: American Psychiatric Publishing.

Chess, S., & Thomas, A. (1984). *Origins and evolution of behavior disorders.* Cambridge, MA: Harvard University Press.

Cohen, J. (1988). *Statistical power analysis for the behavioral sciences.* (2nd ed.). Hillsdale, NJ: Lawrence Erlbaum Associates.

Foley, M., McClowry, S. G., & Castellanos, F. X. (2008). The relationship between attention deficit hyperactivity disorder and child temperament. *Journal of Applied Developmental Psychology, 29,* 157–169.

Gilovich, T., Griffin, D., & Kahneman, D. (Eds.). (2002). *Heuristics and biases: The psychology of intuitive judgment.* New York, NY: Cambridge University Press.

Guerin, D. W., Gottfried, A. W., Oliver, P. H., & Thomas, C. W. (2003). *Temperament: Infancy through adolescence.* New York, NY: Kluwer Academic.

Jensen, P. S., Knapp, P., & Mrazek, D. A. (2006). *Toward a new diagnostic system for child psychopathology. Moving beyond the DSM.* New York, NY: The Guilford Press.

Keogh, B. K. (1994). Temperament and teachers' view of teachability. In W. B. Carey & S. C. McDevitt (Eds.), *Prevention and early intervention: Individual differences as risk factors for the mental health of children: A festschrift for Stella Chess and Alexander Thomas* (pp. 246–254). New York, NY: Brunner/Mazel.

Keogh, B. K. (2003). *Temperament in the classroom: Understanding individual differences.* Baltimore, MD: PH Brookes.

Lyons-Thomas, J., & McClowry, S. G. (2012). An examination of the construct validity and reliability of the Teacher School-Age Temperament Inventory. *Journal of Classroom Interaction, 47*(2), 25–32.

Martin, R. P. (1988). Child temperament and educational outcomes. In A. D. Pelligrini (Ed.), *Psychological bases for early education* (pp. 185–205). New York, NY: Wiley.

Martin, R. P., & Holbrook, J. (1985). Relationship of temperament characteristics to the academic achievement of first-grade children. *Journal of Psychoeducational Assessment, 3*, 131–140.

Martin, R. P., Olejnik, S., & Gaddis, L. (1994). Is temperament an important contributor to schooling outcomes in elementary school? Modeling effects of temperament and scholastic ability on academic achievement. In W. B. Carey & S. C. McDevitt (Eds.), *Prevention and early intervention: Individual differences as risk factors for the mental health of children: A festschrift for Stella Chess and Alexander Thomas* (pp. 59–68). New York, NY: Brunner/Mazel.

McClowry, S. G. (1995). The development of the School-Age Temperament Inventory. *Merrill-Palmer Quarterly, 41*, 271–285.

McClowry, S. G. (2002a). The temperament profiles of school-age children. *Journal of Pediatric Nursing, 17*, 3–10.

McClowry, S. G. (2002b). Transforming temperament profile statistics into puppets and other visual media. *Journal of Pediatric Nursing, 17*, 11–17.

McClowry, S. G., Halverson, C. F., & Sanson, A. (2003). A re-examination of the validity and reliability of the school-age temperament inventory. *Nursing Research, 52*, 176–182.

McClowry, S. G., Rodriguez, E. T., Tamis-LeMonda, C. S., Spellmann, M. E., Carlson, A., & Snow, D. L. (2013). Teacher/student interactions and classroom behavior: The role of student temperament and gender. *Journal of Research in Childhood Education, 27*, 283–301. doi:10.1080/02568543.2013.796330

McClowry, S. G., Snow, D. L., Tamis-LeMonda, C. S., & Rodriguez, E. T. (2010). Testing the efficacy of *INSIGHTS* on student disruptive behavior, classroom management, and student competence in inner city primary grades. *School Mental Health, 2*, 23–35.

McConaughy, S., & Achenbach, T. (1994). Comorbidities of empirically based syndromes in matched general population and clinical samples. *Journal of Child Psychology and Psychiatry, 35*, 1141–1157.

McCormick, M. P., O'Connor, E. E., Cappella, E., & McClowry, S. G. (2014). *Getting a good start in school: Effects of* INSIGHTS *on children with high maintenance temperaments.* Manuscript submitted for publication.

Nardone, G., & Watzlawick, P. (1993). *The art of change: Strategic therapy and hypnotherapy without trance.* San Francisco, CA: Jossey-Bass.

Nunnally, J. C., & Bernstein, I. H. (1994). *Psychometric theory* (3rd ed.). New York, NY: McGraw-Hill.

O'Connor, E. E., Cappella, E., McCormick, M. P., & McClowry, S. G. (in press). Enhancing the academic development of shy children: A test of the efficacy of *INSIGHTS. School Psychology Review.*

Orth, L. C., & Martin, R. P. (1994). Interactive effects of student temperament and instruction method on classroom behavior and achievement. *Journal of School Psychology, 32*(2), 149–166.

Rescorla, L. A., Achenbach, T. M., Ginzburg, S., Ivanova, M., Dumenci, L., Almqvist, F., . . . Verhulst, F. (2007). Consistency of teacher-reported problems for students in 21 countries. *School Psychology Review, 36*(1), 91–110.

Robins, R. W., John, O. P., Caspi, A., Moffitt, T. E., & Stouthamer-Loeber, M. (1996). Resilient, overcontrolled, and undercontrolled boys: Three replicable personality types. *Journal of Personality and Social Psychology, 70*, 157–171.

Rothbart, M., & Bates, J. (2006). Temperament. In W. Damon & R. Lerner (Eds.), *Handbook of Child Psychology: Vol. 3. Social, emotional, and personality development* (6th ed., pp. 99–166). New York, NY: Wiley.

Rudasill, K. M., & Konold, T. R. (2008). Contributions of children's temperament to teachers' judgments of social competence from kindergarten through second grade. *Early Education and Development, 19*(4), 643–666.

Rudasill, K. M., & Rimm-Kaufman, S. E. (2009). Teacher-child relationship quality: The roles of child temperament and teacher–child interactions. *Early Childhood Research Quarterly, 24*(2), 107–120.

Shaffer, D., Fisher, P., Lucas, C., Dulcan, M., & Schwab-Stone, M. (2000). NIMH diagnostic interview schedule for children version IV (NIMH DISC-IV): Description, differences from previous versions, and reliability of some common diagnoses. *Journal of the American Academy of Child and Adolescent Psychiatry, 39*(1), 28–38.

Strelau, J. (2008). *Temperament as a regulator of behavior: After fifty years of research.* Clinton Corners, NY: Eliot Werner.

Watzlawick, P., Weakland, J. H., & Fisch, R. (1974). *Change: Principles of problem formation and problem resolution.* New York, NY: W. W. Norton & Company.

CHAPTER 3

TEACHER RESPONSES

YOU are important to your students! The relationship you have with each of your students matters a great deal. A large number of studies support that conclusion. Individual teachers make an important difference in the adjustment, academic engagement, and achievement of their students (Hamre & Pianta, 2005). The goal of this chapter is to assist you in developing and maintaining caring and supportive relationships with your students.

IN THIS CHAPTER:

- Teacher/student relationships are discussed in light of their impact on student development.

- Various types of interactions that occur between teachers and their students are explored.

- The characteristics of students and teachers that influence teacher feedback are also presented.

- From a temperament perspective, three types of teacher responses— optimal, adequate, and counterproductive—are contrasted.

TEACHER-STUDENT RELATIONSHIPS

A universal need of all humans is to be connected with others. Relationships are indispensable in our lives. Through significant relationships, we learn whether we can trust that others will care for us. The way that we are cared for teaches us how to care for others. Relationships also act like mirrors; they help us understand how we are perceived by others.

Relationships affect both members of a dyad. Multiple transactions provide feedback about the other. These reciprocal and often nuanced interactions affect each member's behavior and attitudes. Over time, patterns of behaviors become established within the dyad that, in turn, influences other important relationships.

Children begin elementary school with several years of relationship experiences. From birth, babies engage in meaningful transactions with their parents and other caregivers. The mother-child relationship is especially important. Intimate early relationships set the stage for the way that children will relate to their elementary school teachers (Mashburn & Pianta, 2006). If a child's early relationships were responsive and provided adequate socialization, the student is advantaged when first meeting his or her kindergarten teacher (Howes & Hamilton, 1992).

Similar to responsive parent-child relationships, good teacher-student relationships involve high levels of closeness and low levels of conflict (Pianta, 1999). The quality of the relationships that children have with their teachers in the early grades influences their interactions with their teachers in subsequent years (Birch & Ladd, 1997; O'Connor, 2010; Pianta, Steinberg, & Rollins, 1995). For example, students who have close and nonconflictual relationships with their primary grade teachers anticipate and often maintain a positive experience with the ones that follow.

Teacher-student relationships continue to contribute to a child's behavioral and academic outcomes throughout the elementary school years, although the degree of closeness between students and their teachers decreases gradually as peer relationships become more important (O'Connor, 2010). Still, positive relationships between students and their teachers in the upper elementary grades are protective and reduce the likelihood that students will develop adjustment problems (O'Connor, Dearing, & Collins, 2011).

Even one low-quality relationship with a teacher can have long-term repercussions that result in lower student achievement (O'Connor & McCartney, 2007). If, however, a subsequent teacher has a better relationship with the student, it, too, can have a profound effect (O'Connor & McCartney, 2007). A warm and supportive teacher-student relationship can reduce the internalizing and externalizing student behavior problems of children (O'Connor et al., 2011).

A meta-analysis of over one hundred studies supports that the quality of teacher-student relationship is central to classroom management (Marzano, Marzano, & Pickering, 2003). Low-quality teacher relationships are associated with aggressive and withdrawn student behavior (O'Connor et al., 2011). In contrast, teachers who have good relationships with their students have fewer classroom discipline problems, and their students exhibit fewer rule violations (Pianta et al., 1995).

Positive teacher-student relationships are particularly important for disadvantaged minority children (O'Connor, 2010). Children from families experiencing a number of stressors and students who have less than optimal relationships with their parents particularly gravitate toward their teachers. Positive relationship with their teacher can be healing for the children (Howes & Ritchie, 1999). Together the aforementioned studies confirm that teachers have an especially important role in the lives of their disadvantaged students.

INTERACTIONS BETWEEN TEACHERS AND THEIR STUDENTS

Teachers and students affect each other in dynamic ways. Every day, a plethora of events occur in classrooms requiring teachers to respond to student requests and to their behavior. Many of these events are, from the viewpoint of the teacher, routine. From the perspective of a student, however, the situations often take on a much larger significance because they occur within the context of the teacher-student relationship.

Dramatic differences exist in the way that teachers interact with their students. Responsive teachers are flexible (Hamre & Pianta, 2005). Their interactions are warm, yet relay clear expectations for classroom behavior (Brody, Dorsey, Forehand, & Armistead, 2002). When infractions occur, students can expect that fair consequences will follow.

On the other hand, ineffective teachers use punitive and coercive discipline in response to student behavior problems even when their strategies don't work (Pullis, 1985). A classroom observation study by Nelson and Roberts (2000) clearly illustrates how teacher and student interactions influence each other and affect their overall relationships. Nelson and Roberts asked teachers to identify students in their elementary school classrooms who were disruptive and others who were typical, but not optimal. Classroom observations showed that when a disruptive behavior occurred, teachers responded differently to the two types of students. When a typical student was disruptive, teachers issued a request for the student to act appropriately such as, "Please read your book quietly." If, however, the same type of behavior was exhibited by a student who was targeted as disruptive, the teachers were more likely to issue a stern reprimand, such as "Stop that hitting now."

The two types of students in the Nelson and Roberts study (2000) differed in their responses to their teachers' directives. Typical students almost always complied after the first teacher command was issued. The disruptive students, however, did not. Then in reaction to their noncompliance, the teachers issued another reprimand, which usually was followed by another incident of disruptive student behavior. The pattern of teacher commands and student disruptive behavior continued to spiral, escalating without a successful resolution. Nelson and Roberts concluded that repeating the same command to a disruptive student exacerbates rather than resolves the problem student behavior. Moreover, noncompliance by the disruptive student frustrates and annoys the teacher—and the deleterious interactional pattern goes on and on and on . . .

Unless some intentional action interrupts the cycle, yesterday's exchanges between a student and teacher are likely to shape today's interaction, and will probably be reflected in future encounters. By understanding the feedback mechanisms that teachers use in their transactions with students, deliberate efforts can be made to respond in more effective ways. The literature attaches a number of labels to the various ways that teachers respond to their students. In general, the types of feedback can be categorized as positive or negative. Positive feedback is warm, affirming teacher behavior that relays approval. Negative teacher feedback includes critical or disparaging comments or nonverbal behaviors.

Teachers are often surprised (and, understandably disappointed) to learn that a great deal of teacher feedback is harsh (Jones & Dindia, 2004). Many classroom observation studies have documented that teachers provide much more negative than positive feedback to their students (McClowry et al., 2013). In addition, teachers are more likely to respond to inappropriate student actions than to acknowledge appropriate student behavior (Beaman & Wheldall, 2000).

Too few instances of positive feedback occur in many classrooms. When positive teacher feedback does occur, it often is in response to academic rather than social behavior (Beaman & Wheldall, 2000). Moreover, teachers tend to be positive with students that they perceive as sensitive to their feedback while ignoring or reprimanding those they regard as disruptive (Glen, Heath, Karagiannakis, & Hoida, 2004).

HOW STUDENT CHARACTERISTICS ARE RELATED TO TEACHER FEEDBACK

Teachers respond differently to their students depending on a child's personal characteristics and past behavior. Students who are disruptive receive a great deal of negative feedback. Sutherland (2000) found that emotionally disturbed students receive six times more negative than positive feedback. Yet, as previously discussed, frequent critical feedback to disruptive students heightens rather than reduces problem behavior. In addition, it adversely affects the teacher/student relationship (Sutherland, 2000).

Gender is another characteristic of students that has been studied in relationship to teacher feedback. Meta-analyses have found no differences in the amount of positive feedback that teachers provide boys and girls (Jones & Dindia, 2004). Ironically, however, girls who exhibit behavior particularly valued by teachers receive less attention than boys (Kelly, 1988).

Negative interactions between teachers and the boys and girls in their classrooms show a definitive pattern. Elementary school teachers perceive their relationships with their male students as more conflictual than with their female students (Rudasill, Gallagher, & White, 2010). Teachers interact more with boys (Jones & Dindia, 2004), but their interactions tend to be more managerial, disciplinary, and negative, which serves to increase rather than decrease the boys' problem behavior patterns (Lindow, Marrett, & Wilkinson, 1985). One of the major reasons that teachers interact more with boys than girls is because, in general, male students are more disruptive and, thereby, prompt more response from their teachers (Jones & Dindia, 2004). For example, boys are more likely to call out their answers in response to their teachers' questions, whereas girls usually raise their hands.

Although the number of teacher interactions with boys compared to girls is not large during any one given year, the amount becomes substantial over the course of the elementary school years. Kelly (1988) estimates that boys receive 1,800 more hours of teacher attention in elementary school than girls. Student gender, however, is only part of the story. After conducting a meta-analysis of eighty-eight studies examining gender differences in teacher feedback, Kelly (1988) concluded that because gender produces only a small effect size, other student characteristics must play a part.

A recent study identified temperament as another contributing factor (McClowry et al., 2013). Regardless of gender, students whose temperaments are high maintenance were more likely than industrious students to receive negative feedback from their teachers. Students with high maintenance temperaments received eight times more negative than positive feedback.

In another study, students in middle school with challenging temperaments had more conflict with their teachers than those with easier temperaments (Rudasill, Reio, Stipanovic, & Taylor, 2010). Both studies demonstrate that student temperament plays an important role in type and amount of teacher feedback. Given the importance of relationships between teachers and students, it is also important to consider how teacher characteristics are related to the feedback students receive.

HOW TEACHER CHARACTERISTICS ARE RELATED TO TEACHER FEEDBACK

The characteristics of teachers affect their classroom interactions. One characteristic that might be expected to contribute to the quality of teacher-student relationships is the teacher's own temperament or personality. Unfortunately, the topic has received little investigation. In one of the few studies that have examined teacher personality, Yoon (2002) found that teachers who were high in negative reactivity, compared to those who were low, had less-positive relationships with their students. They also had lower perceptions of their own self-efficacy in classroom management. Self-efficacy is the perception that one is capable of handling a situation to achieve a goal (Bandura, 1991). Simply stated, individuals act more decisively when they perceive themselves as efficacious.

Teachers who view themselves as efficacious in classroom management are more adept at managing challenging student behaviors (Baker, 2005) and are more flexible in the strategies they use when conflict occurs in their classrooms (Morris-Rothschild & Brassard, 2006). They also have warmer relationships with their students (O'Connor, 2010), more positive perceptions of their students (McClowry et al., 2013), and experience less job-related stress (Mashburn & Pianta, 2006).

Students appreciate when their teachers are effective in maintaining a classroom conducive to learning and creating an environment in which they feel safe. The results from focus groups of students in grades 4 to 7 illustrate these points; students expressed a preference for definitive teachers who were efficacious in classroom management rather than those who were permissive (Chiu & Tulley, 1997).

One of the ways that you can increase your own self-efficacy in classroom management is by learning effective ways to respond to people in your life. The following section explains how you can use a temperament lens to interpret your interactions. Such insight can enhance relationships with your students and promote your success as a teacher.

FROM A TEMPERAMENT PERSPECTIVE:
TYPES OF TEACHER RESPONSES

Temperament theory provides an intriguing lens from which to interpret teacher-student relationships. A myriad of circumstances—a scheduled examination, an approaching vacation, or a postponed field trip, to mention only a few examples—prompt temperamental reactions from students. The circumstances to which a particular student reacts and the manifestations of that reaction are usually consistent with a child's temperament: Hilary the Hard Worker might be excited about conducting a class science project while Gregory the Grumpy might find the assignment boring. As the project evolves, however, other reactions may occur. Hilary might become upset if she does not have enough time to finish the project or if she thinks that her work does not meet her own high expectations. Gregory, on the other hand, might complain that the project is taking too long and is interfering with other activities in which he would rather be engaged. In another part of the classroom, Coretta the Cautious is likely to find working on the science assignment more comfortable if her project partner is her best friend. In contrast, Freddy the Friendly might enjoy the opportunity to work with a new classmate and be less concerned about the quality of the final project.

As figure 3.1 illustrates, a student will usually react to one of these "life happens" situations in a way that is consistent with his or her temperament. The teacher, in turn, can respond to the student's reaction in a variety of ways. Some teacher responses are more effective than are others. In this chapter, three categories of teacher responses, *counterproductive*, *adequate*, and *optimal* are discussed. Several examples of each will be presented.

> *Counterproductive:* A teacher response that only makes the situation worse. Usually counterproductive responses are delivered in an angry tone of voice.
> *Adequate:* A teacher response that is intended to get the situation resolved quickly and is spoken in a neutral fashion.
> *Optimal:* A response in which the teacher tries to enhance the competency of the student. Optimal responses often recognize the individuality of the child by acknowledging his or her temperamental tendencies or other attributes. Optimal statements are relayed in a warm, understanding manner that is not judgmental. Rather it is accepting.

Notice that the way the response is delivered is an integral component of the message. Statements that acknowledge the individuality of the child, but that are delivered

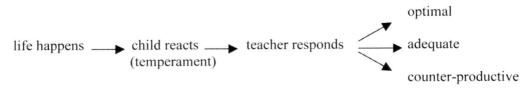

life happens ⟶ child reacts ⟶ teacher responds ⟶ optimal / adequate / counter-productive
(temperament)

Figure 3.1

harshly, relay a mixed message. Likewise, negative statements that are said with a smile generate an equally confusing message. Mixed messages are ineffective and can be hurtful because children typically internalize only the negative tone and do not hear the positive statement.

Counterproductive Responses. Teacher responses can easily become counterproductive when even a minor event escalates into a negative spiral of reactivity between a teacher and a student. For example, preparing for the daily school dismissal can be a stressful time and may elicit a number of temperamental reactions from students, which, in turn, may prompt teacher responses. Consider what might happen if Gregory, who is high in negative reactivity, cannot find his math book just when it is time to line up at the door to meet the school bus. Missing textbooks constitute a "life happens" situation that will challenge Gregory and his teacher. At 2:55 p.m.—with a 3:00 p.m. dismissal rapidly approaching—counterproductive responses can easily occur:

BOX 3.1. Life Happens: A Counterproductive Teacher Response

Ms. Davis: Okay, students, before you line up at the door, check your backpacks to make sure that you have your math workbook for tonight's homework.

Gregory: Ms. Davis! Ms. Davis! I can't find my math workbook.

Ms. Davis: Do you remember where you last put it?

Gregory: If I remembered, would I be asking you?

Ms. Davis: That is no way to talk to me, young man. If you would put your things in your desk where they belong, you would find them. And we wouldn't have to deal with your problems. I don't know why you do this!

Gregory: You don't have to yell at me for nothing!

Ms. Davis: For nothing? You need to put your school materials away where they belong! If you did, you wouldn't be running into this problem. And I will not have you speak to me that way.

In response to her student's temperamental reaction, "If I remembered, would I be asking you?" Gregory's teacher reacted with a *counterproductive* statement. She lectured him about "putting his things away." As illustrated in the scenario, her counterproductive response just made the situation worse. Such responses are especially ineffective with children, like Gregory, who are high in negative reactivity because they trigger a negative spiral of reactivity that does nothing to resolve the problem. If Gregory and his teacher continue to interact, it is likely that Gregory would raise his voice even louder with each subsequent statement, as would his teacher. By the time their verbal battle is completed, Gregory and his teacher are guaranteed to be frustrated with each other, especially as the school dismissal time becomes more imminent and finding the math workbook becomes more critical. Teachers whose own temperaments are high in

Table 3.1. Counterproductive Teacher Responses

Nagging	Repeating the same message over and over.
Lecturing	A scolding that goes on and on and often includes a discussion of previous mistakes the child has made.
Withdrawal	A passive and ineffective response that is indifferent to the student and ineffective in assisting the child to solve the dilemma. (As will be discussed in greater detail later, withdrawal is different than "ignoring," which if done intentionally can be very effective.)
Hassled	An irritated response spoken while the teacher is paying attention to another student or doing something else.
Teasing	Talking to the student in a way that taunts or teases the child or includes sarcasm.
Nattering	A nonverbal expression of teacher displeasure that does not deal with the student's behavior directly. Instead, the teacher makes a face or uses a gesture, like shrugging his or her shoulders or saying something sarcastic about the child. A nattering response can also be a negative comment said about the student to someone else while the child is listening.

negative reactivity are particularly prone to engaging in negative spirals of reactivity that escalate the transactions. Table 3.1 lists several types of counterproductive responses.

Counterproductive responses compromise the classroom environment in a number of ways. They are ineffective in handling a student's noncompliance. Instead they relay an uncaring response to the child that, when used repeatedly, will adversely affect the student-teacher relationship. Counterproductive teacher responses also contribute to the negative spiral of reactivity that results in escalating student noncompliance into deviance.

All teachers periodically use a counterproductive response. The ability to self-identify the use of a counterproductive reply is a critical first step in reducing the occurrences of negative interactions by replacing them with more effective responses. Adequate and optimal statements put the teacher in charge of the situation and the classroom.

Adequate Teacher Responses. *Adequate* teacher responses are recommended for most situations. The intent of such responses is to resolve a situation quickly and effectively. When using such responses, the teacher relays the expectation that the student will be compliant so that the situation can be resolved. Such teacher responses are "adequate" because they convey that members of the community treat each other with mutual respect and courtesy. Table 3.2 lists several types of adequate responses.

If Gregory's teacher had used an adequate response when her class was getting ready to be dismissed at the end of the school day, it is likely that the scenario would have progressed in a different fashion. For example, Gregory's teacher may have taken command by matter-of-factly responding with:

BOX 3.2. LIFE HAPPENS: AN ADEQUATE TEACHER RESPONSE

Gregory: Ms. Davis! Ms. Davis! I can't find my math workbook.
Ms. Davis: It's under your desk.

Table 3.2. Adequate Teacher Responses

Taking Command	Giving a student or the class a directive using clear, simple language.
Humor	A jovial but caring response. When humor is used sincerely, it can lighten a situation and prompt a resolution.
Cooling Down	Being calm when a student or when the whole classroom is overexcited. Cooling down is particularly effective when said with a slow, quiet voice.
Signal	A quiet warning given to a student or the class.
Ignore	An intentional effort to ignore a particular student's behavior. (Ignoring is especially useful for remarks made by students who are high in negative reactivity.)

Using an adequate response was a good choice for Ms. Davis because Gregory's temperament is high in negativity. She is trying to get the situation resolved without it escalating. Given the time pressures involved in getting the students in line for meeting the school bus, a straightforward answer can be effective in quickly resolving an issue.

Two types of adequate responses require further explanation. Teachers are encouraged to adopt and consistently use a *signal*—a strategy that is effective as a first-step disciplinary strategy for a challenging student or for the entire classroom. Different types of signals and how to use them effectively are explained in greater detail in chapter 4.

Ignoring is another powerful adequate teacher response (Baden & Howe, 1992; Patterson, 1982). One point, regarding ignoring, cannot be stressed enough: effective teachers demonstrate a great deal of discretion in determining when to respond and when to ignore a situation or comment. Ineffective teachers, on the other hand, overreact to trivial situations that are best ignored. Rather than neutralizing a student-initiated negative interaction, ineffective teachers escalate it by using counterproductive responses, such as reacting in an irritated manner.

Determining when to ignore and when to get involved requires good judgment. If there is a concern about a student's safety, of course, a teacher must get involved. In other circumstances, particularly those that are attention-seeking and that are not destructive, ignoring can be an appropriate strategy. For example, a student might be whining because, from her perspective, too much homework has been assigned. An effective teacher may briefly acknowledge the student's comment or may just ignore it. In either case, an effective teacher will continue to ignore the student's comments, even if the student increases the volume of his or her complaints.

Under no circumstances, however, does ignoring allow a teacher to abdicate her or his monitoring role. Instead the teacher continues to discreetly observe what is going on with the child, but intentionally does not react or even respond unless the student's behavior becomes unsafe. For example, minor squabbles between classmates should be ignored if the students are old enough to resolve their own disagreements. A statement such as, "I know that the two of you can decide who will use the computer first without needing my help" is another appropriate adequate response. Still, the vigilant teacher should remain attentive to what is going on between students to assure that one is not taking advantage of the other, but that a balanced resolution has occurred.

From a temperament perspective, ignoring is an indispensable teacher strategy to use when a student's temperament is high in negative reactivity. Because one cannot remake a student who is high in negative reactivity into a sunny individual, teachers need to be judicious in selecting times to negotiate with the student versus times when ignoring should be used. Well-intentioned teachers who appreciate the importance of negotiating with their students may inadvertently encourage a child who is high in negativity to become a disruptive influence in the classroom. If a teacher responds to every negative comment by attempting to soothe the child, the student becomes very powerful. Such students quickly learn that they can control their teacher or classmates by constantly expressing their distress.

Some teachers whose own temperaments are high in negative reactivity may find ignoring particularly difficult to implement. Such teachers react rather than respond. Teachers who are aware of their reaction style can decisively implement more effective teaching strategies, like adequate strategies and those that are optimal.

Optimal Teacher Responses. *Optimal* teacher responses are intended to foster a student's competency, not just to gain his or her compliance. By definition, optimal responses are relayed with warmth while still asserting expectations for responsible behavior. One type of optimal response is to encourage a student to problem-solve a "life happens" event. In contrast to an adequate teacher response in which your directive is intended to resolve the situation, an optimal response engages the student in exploring possible solutions. Encouraging the student to problem-solve supports his or her sense of competence and independence.

A second kind of optimal response acknowledges that you have heard a student's comment, but circumstances or expectations for behavior require that you deny his or her request. For example, a student may request that the class play soccer at recess. An optimal response could be, "I wish that the class could go out at recess today, but it's raining. Instead, I hope that. . . . " The first part of the statement, "I wish" tells the student that you have heard him or her. The "but" portion of the interchange reasserts teacher control and guidance.

A third type of optimal response tells the student that although you are sensitive to his or her reaction, the situation requires a response that may be somewhat uncomfortable. For example, you might say to a student who is high in withdrawal,

Table 3.3. Optimal Teacher Responses Related to Child Temperament

Temperamental Tendency		Examples of Optimal Responses
Task persistence	High task persistence	"I know you would prefer to continue reading right now, but it's time for us to move on to our science lesson. You can come back to your book this afternoon during choice time."
	Low task persistence	"I know this assignment is difficult, but I want you to work really hard for fifteen minutes and then it will be time to go to lunch."
Withdrawal	High withdrawal	"I know that you would prefer to first watch the other children rather than join in, so let me stand with you a few minutes until you feel ready to work with them."
	Low withdrawal	"I know you are curious, but it is not safe for you to wander around the museum by yourself."
Activity	High activity	"I know you like to be active, but you need to be careful in the classroom so that you do not bump into the other students."
	Low activity	"I know you prefer quiet activities, but we made a class decision that we're going to have a basketball tournament on the playground today."
Reactivity	High negative reactivity	An optimal teacher response to a child high in negative reactivity is to refrain from reacting in an intense, negative way that will only serve to escalate the situation. Instead use adequate responses.
	Low negative reactivity	"I know it's easy for you to go along with the ideas of your friends, but are you sure that this is something you want to do?"

"I understand that you might find it challenging to give an oral report, but I will help you prepare for the assignment." Such a statement is not intended to change the child's temperament but offers support while he or she navigates a course of action that requires stretching his or her temperamental tendencies. Table 3.3 lists optimal statements that are related to a child's temperament. Notice that many of these examples also use the "but" convention to relay teacher expectations for behavior.

If you have not previously used optimal teacher responses, try one out. You may find that, at first, optimal statements may startle your students because they deeply communicate that you recognize and appreciate their individuality. The surprise, however, will be a pleasant one for you and your students.

The effective use of optimal responses and other strategies from temperament-based classroom management requires knowing when to use them and how often.

Optimal statements are best reserved for moments when there is adequate time for the teacher and the child to engage in an interaction that fosters the child's development. For example, Gregory's teacher might have responded with an optimal statement if enough time was available to resolve the missing math workbook. The scenario could have proceeded in the following manner:

BOX 3.3. SO CAN STUDENTS WHO ARE VERY ENERGETIC

Gregory: Ms. Davis! Ms. Davis! I can't find my math workbook.
Ms. Davis: If I remember correctly, you and Susan were using the book this morning to catch up on some pages you both missed when you were sick earlier this week. Do you remember where you were working?

As with other powerful techniques, optimal responses should be used judiciously. The overuse of optimal statements decreases their effectiveness. When employed constantly, students become bored with them and the optimal statements become ineffective. The same statement can be made regarding praise as discussed in box 3.5, "An FYI on Praise."

Of course, there is no guarantee that using an optimal teacher response will result in a positive resolution. Even if Gregory's teacher used an optimal statement that encouraged him to resolve his own problem, Gregory might have reacted negatively. Yet, while optimal statements do not always produce successful interactions, counterproductive responses, most assuredly, lead to calamitous consequences.

A FAMILIAR SCENARIO, "HE PUSHED ME"

Another scenario occurs at some time or another with students of every temperament. As all teachers know, pushing between classmates can happen at any moment. The teacher strategies used for "He (or she) pushed me" will depend on the context in which it occurs. A minor shoving incident is different from one that is highly aggressive and is intended to seriously hurt another student. Another factor is the size of the students. Even a shove can be more dangerous when students become older and stronger. In such cases, a teacher needs to respond assertively to maintain a safe school environment. The following example, however, is intended to portray the annoying behavior that students sometimes exhibit when they are hassling, not hurting each other. Children who are high in negative reactivity are particularly likely to engage in such encounters.

In this scenario, Gregory and Freddy are working on a computer exercise, when an outbreak of "He pushed me" occurs. Assume that Ms. Davis saw the minor altercation and noted that neither boy got hurt. There are a number of ways that Ms. Davis can handle the "life happens" situation. As you read the following examples, try to identify whether her responses are counterproductive, adequate, or optimal.

BOX 3.4. EXAMPLE 1

Freddy: Ms. Davis! Gregory pushed me.
Ms. Davis: All right, Gregory and Freddy. If you boys cannot work together peacefully, then you will need to collect your own materials and work separately.

BOX 3.5. AN FYI ON PRAISE

Teachers often assume that praise is a type of teacher feedback that results in positive outcomes with children. After a comprehensive review of the literature on praise and intrinsic motivation, Henderlong and Lepper (2002) arrive at a more nuanced conclusion. Under some conditions, praise promotes beneficial effects that enhance a child's intrinsic motivation and perseverance. Inappropriate uses, however, dampen autonomy and competence. For example, praising a student for completing an easy task conveys to a child that your expectations regarding his or her ability are low.

Overuse and nonspecific use of praise also increase the likelihood that children will become dependent on positive feedback from adults rather than developing their own internalized standard for performance and behavior. However, when used judiciously and selectively, praise can enhance the autonomy of children. Praise is best used when directed at a student process ("You worked really hard on that assignment.") rather than in regard to a personal attribute or ability ("You are really good at solving logic problems.").

Culture influences the use of praise that children receive at home. Henderlong and Lepper (2002) explain that parents in collectivistic cultures, such as in Asian communities, seldom praise their children. Instead they expect compliance and are more focused on the family or community unit as a whole than on individuals.

Researchers also found that some African American parents prefer more neutral terminology such as "recognition" or "acknowledgment" rather than the word "praise" in describing how they provide positive feedback to their children (Tamis-LeMonda, Briggs, McClowry, & Snow, 2008). Regardless of whether positive feedback is labeled praise, recognition, or reinforcement, students need it because it clarifies that their behavior meets the teacher's expectation. When you praise students, be sincere and specific in your comments.

Ms. Davis took control of the situation with an adequate response. She resolved the issue in a matter-of-fact way by reminding the boys of a negative consequence that would follow if they could not get along with each other.

BOX 3.6. EXAMPLE 2

Freddy: Ms. Davis! Gregory pushed me.

Ms. Davis: Maybe Gregory didn't mean it? Sometimes kids bump into each other while they are working on the computer because there isn't much space. Did he say he was sorry or did he try to get out of your way?

In this example, Ms. Davis uses an adequate response that she hopes will cool down the situation. Her comments try to help Freddy reframe the event in a more benign way so that the situation does not escalate.

BOX 3.7. EXAMPLE 3

Freddy: Ms. Davis! Gregory pushed me.

Ms. Davis: Gregory, why did you do that to Freddy? When are you boys going to learn how to work together without fighting? You two are always fighting.

The counterproductive response that Ms. Davis uses this time is lecturing. Notice also that Ms. Davis does not take any decisive action to correct the situation.

BOX 3.8. EXAMPLE 4

Freddy: Ms. Davis! Gregory pushed me.

Ms. Davis: Sometimes when children are working together, it's easy to get in each other's way. Maybe you guys need to give each other more room. How could you give each other more space and still get your assignment done?

This teacher response is optimal because Ms. Davis tries to assist the boys to resolve the problem themselves.

BOX 3.9. EXAMPLE 5

Freddy: Ms. Davis! Gregory pushed me.

Ms. Davis: I saw what happened. You pushed him and then he pushed you. You are just trying to get him in trouble. You always think that everyone is picking on you, but it's you that always starts the fights. I don't know what to do with you, Freddy. Why can't you kids get along?

Ms. Davis uses another counterproductive response—this time by nagging Freddy. If, in turn, Freddy tries to defend himself, it's unlikely to help because the initial response of Ms. Davis began so negatively.

BOX 3.10. EXAMPLE 6

Freddy: Ms. Davis! Gregory pushed me.

Ms. Davis: (sighs and shrugs)

In this instance, Ms. Davis demonstrates a nattering counterproductive response. She neither acknowledges Freddy nor acts decisively to resolve the situation.

BOX 3.11. EXAMPLE 7

Freddy: Ms. Davis! Gregory pushed me.

Ms. Davis: Gregory, come here. All right, boys, what are the rules of our classroom regarding working together?

This teacher response was optimal because Ms. Davis engages the boys in resolving the situation by having them remind each other of the classroom rules.

BOX 3.12. EXAMPLE 8

Freddy: Ms. Davis! Gregory pushed me.

Ms. Davis: Ms. Davis! Gregory pushed me. Ms. Davis! I'm a baby. I can't handle my own problems.

The previous response was blatantly counterproductive. Ms. Davis ineffectively responded to the situation by teasing and taunting Freddy. In response, Freddy is likely to feel misunderstood and may conclude that his teacher will not assist him when he encounters other difficult situations.

BOX 3.13. EXAMPLE 9

Freddy: Ms. Davis! Gregory pushed me.
Ms. Davis: (looks away and gives no response)

The passive, withdrawn response of Ms. Davis is counterproductive. Freddy is likely to escalate his complaints until he gets her attention.

BOX 3.14. EXAMPLE 10

Freddy: Ms. Davis! Gregory pushed me.
Ms. Davis: Freddy and Gregory! We do not allow pushing in our classroom. If one of you pushes the other again, I will send you both back to your desks and you will have to work on the assignment without using a computer.

Ms. Davis demonstrates an adequate teacher response. She clearly states her expectations for behavior and the consequences that will follow if they are not compliant.

BOX 3.15. EXAMPLE 11

Freddy: Ms. Davis! Gregory pushed me.
Ms. Davis: Freddy, can't you see I'm busy?

The hassled response that Ms. Davis exhibits is counterproductive and does not address, let alone resolve, the pushing incident at all.

BOX 3.16. EXAMPLE 12

Freddy: Ms. Davis! Gregory pushed me.
Ms. Davis: How are you and Gregory going to resolve this issue?

Engaging in a discussion of "who pushed who" and "why" is likely to make the situation worse. Instead, Ms. Davis uses an optimal response by attempting to get the boys to resolve their own problems.

Now that you have had an opportunity to observe the responses of Ms. Davis, it is time to focus on your own. Reflect on your own temperament. What is your perception regarding your own level of negative reactivity? Are you high, low, or intermediate? Think about how your own level of negative reactivity influences your responses with children and adults.

SUMMARY

In this chapter caring and supportive teacher-student relationships are credited with fostering students' social and academic development and in enhancing classroom management. Positive teacher-student relationships, especially in the primary grades, have long-term repercussions for a student's academic and behavioral outcomes. Economically disadvantaged minority students particularly benefit from such relationships. Responsive teachers are warm yet effective in dealing with classroom management.

In general, teachers provide much more negative than positive feedback to their students. When they offer positive feedback, it tends to be related to academic matters rather than the student's behavior. Disruptive students receive more attention from their teachers, but the feedback they receive is usually negative and only serves to escalate the student's disruptive behavior. Teachers also give more negative feedback to students with high maintenance temperaments, regardless of whether they are boys or girls, compared to those with less challenging temperaments.

Teachers with higher self-efficacy are effective in managing student behavior and have better relationships with their students. Three types of teacher responses are explicated as influencing student behavior and teacher-student relationships. Counterproductive teacher responses are delivered in an angry tone of voice and usually make the situation worse. An adequate teacher response is intended to get the situation resolved quickly and is spoken in a neutral fashion. Optimal teacher responses aim to enhance the competency of a student and are relayed in a warm, understanding manner.

In the next chapter, scaffolding is introduced as way to enhance the social-emotional development of students. Recommendations for structuring the classroom context before the school year begins are offered. Then a variety of strategies for maintaining a supportive classroom are presented.

CLASS DISCUSSION

- Make a Popsicle-stick teacher. Be creative in how you create your teacher. Use the Popsicle-stick teacher and the Popsicle-stick students you made in chapter 2 to role-play the following scenarios. In each situation, have your teacher give an optimal, adequate, and counterproductive response:
  - The class period is almost over. Gregory asks to use the restroom again—even though he just used it thirty minutes ago.
  - Hilary is upset. She says she finished her homework but forgot to bring it to school.

  o Freddy has successfully gotten all of the students (even Coretta) joining the "chicken dance" while the students were lining up for lunch.
  o Coretta says her stomach hurts so she cannot do her class presentation.
- Create your own scenarios and role-play them with your Popsicle people.

OPTIONAL CASE STUDY ASSIGNMENT

Now that you have had an opportunity to observe the responses of Ms. Davis, it is time to focus on your own. Before you begin to observe your responses, reflect on your own temperament. What is your intuitive impression regarding your own level of negative reactivity? Are you high, low, or intermediate? As you observe your responses to your students, how does your level of negative reactivity influence your responses? The following exercise is intended to help you answer that question.

Case Study Assignment 3: Observing Your Own Teacher Responses

Consider the following questions:

1. Everyone uses a counterproductive response now and then. Can you remember one that you used? Please describe it.
2. How did the student react to your counterproductive response?
3. Describe an adequate response that you have used.
4. How did the student react?
5. Use an optimal statement with a student and then record it.
6. How did the student react?

RECOMMENDED READINGS

McClowry, S. G., Rodriguez, E. T., Tamis-LeMonda, C. S., Spellmann, M. E., Carlson, A., & Snow, D. L. (2013). Teacher/student interactions and classroom behavior: The role of student temperament and gender. *Journal of Research in Childhood Education, 27,* 283–301. doi:10.1080/02568543.2013.796330

Nelson, J. R., & Roberts, M. L. (2000). Ongoing reciprocal teacher-student interactions involving disruptive behaviors in general education classrooms. *Journal of Emotional and Behavioral Disorders, 8,* 27–37. doi:10.1177/106342660000800104

O'Connor, E. (2010). Teacher-child relationships as dynamic systems. *Journal of School Psychology, 48,* 187–218. doi:10.1016/j.jsp.2010.01.001

REFERENCES

Baden, A. D., & Howe, G. W. (1992). Mothers' attributions and expectancies regarding their conduct-disordered children. *Journal of Abnormal Child Psychology, 20*(5), 467–485. doi:10.1007/BF00916810

Baker, P. H. (2005). Managing student behavior: How ready are teachers to meet the challenge? *American Secondary Education, 33*(3), 51–64.

Bandura, A. (1991). Social cognitive theory of self-regulation. *Organizational Behavior and Human Decision Processes, 50,* 248–268. doi:10.1016/0749-5978(91)90022-L

Beaman, R., & Wheldall, K. (2000). Teachers' use of approval and disapproval in the classroom. *Educational Psychology, 20*(4), 431–446. doi:10.1080/713663753

Birch, S. H., & Ladd, G. W. (1997). The teacher-child relationship and children's early school adjustment. *Journal of School Psychology, 35,* 61–79. doi:10.1016/S0022-4405(96)00029-5

Brody, G. H., Dorsey, S., Forehand, R., & Armistead, L. (2002). Unique and protective contributions of parenting and classroom processes to the adjustment of African American children living in single-parent families. *Child Development, 73,* 274–286. doi:10.1111/1467-8624.00405

Chiu, L. H., & Tulley, M. (1997). Student preferences of teacher discipline styles. *Journal of Instructional Psychology, 24*(3), 168–175.

Glen, T., Heath, N. L., Karagiannakis, A., & Hoida, D. (2004). Feedback practices in a sample of children with emotional and/or behavioral difficulties: The relationship between teacher and child perceptions of feedback frequency and the role of child sensitivity. *Emotional & Behavioural Difficulties, 9*(1), 54–69. doi:10.1177/1363275204041963

Hamre, B. K., & Pianta, R. C. (2005). Can instructional and emotional support in the first-grade classroom make a difference for children at risk of school failure? *Child Development, 76*(5), 949–967. doi:10.1111/j.1467-8624.2005.00889.x

Henderlong, J., & Lepper, M. R. (2002). The effects of praise on children's intrinsic motivation: A review and synthesis. *Psychological Bulletin, 128*(5), 774–795. doi:10.1037//0033-2909.128.5.774

Howes, C., & Hamilton, C. E. (1992). Children's relationships with child care teachers: Stability and concordance with parental attachment. *Child Development, 63,* 867–878. doi:10.2307/1131239

Howes, C., & Ritchie, S. (1999). Attachment organizations in children with difficult life circumstances. *Development and Psychopathology, 11,* 251–268. doi:10.1017/S0954579499002047

Jerome, E. M., Hamre, B. K., & Pianta, R. C. (2009). Teacher-child relationships from kindergarten to sixth grade: Early childhood predictors of teacher-perceived conflict and closeness. *Social Development, 18*(4), 915–945. doi:10.1111/j.1467-9507.2008.00508.x

Jones, S. M., & Dindia, K. (2004). A meta-analytic perspective on sex equity in the classroom. *Review of Educational Research, 74*(4), 443–471. doi:10.3102/00346543074004443

Kelly, A. (1988). Gender differences in teacher-pupil interactions: A meta-analytic review. *Research in Education, 39,* 1–23.

Lindow, J., Marrett, C. B., & Wilkinson, L. C. (1985). Overview. In L. C. Wilkinson and C. B. Marrett (Eds.), *Gender Influences in Classroom Instruction* (pp. 1–15). Orlando: Academic Press, Inc.

Marzano, R. J., Marzano, J. S., & Pickering, D. J. (2003). *Classroom management that works: Research-based strategies for every teacher.* Alexandria, VA: Association for Supervision and Curriculum Development.

Mashburn, A. J., & Pianta, R. C. (2006). Social relationships and school readiness. *Early Education and Development, 17*(1), 151–176. doi:10.1207/s15566935eed1701_7

McClowry, S. G., Rodriguez, E. T., Tamis-LeMonda, C. S., Spellmann, M. E., Carlson, A., & Snow, D. L. (2013). Teacher/student interactions and classroom behavior: The role of student temperament and gender. *Journal of Research in Childhood Education, 27,* 283–301. doi:10.1080/02568543.2013.796330

Morris-Rothschild, B. K., & Brassard, M. R. (2006). Teachers' conflict management styles: The role of attachment styles and classroom management efficacy. *Journal of School Psychology, 44*, 105–121. doi:10.1016/j.jsp.2006.01.004

Nelson, J. R., & Roberts, M. L. (2000). Ongoing reciprocal teacher-student interactions involving disruptive behaviors in general education classrooms. *Journal of Emotional and Behavioral Disorders, 8*, 27–37. doi:10.1177/106342660000800104

O'Connor, E. (2010). Teacher-child relationships as dynamic systems. *Journal of School Psychology, 48*, 187–218. doi:10.1016/j.jsp.2010.01.001

O'Connor, E., Dearing, E., & Collins, B. (2011). Teacher-child relationship trajectories: Predictors of behavior problem trajectories and mediators of child and family factors. *American Educational Research Journal, 48*(1), 120–162. doi:10.3102/0002831210365008

O'Connor, E., & McCartney, K. (2007). Examining teacher-child relationships and achievement as part of an ecological model of development. *American Educational Research Journal, 44*, 340–369. doi:10.3102/0002831207302172

Patterson, G. R. (1982). *Coercive family process.* Eugene, OR: Castalia.

Pianta, R. C. (1999). *Enhancing relationships between children and teachers.* Washington, DC: American Psychological Association.

Pianta, R. C., Steinberg, M. S., & Rollins, K. B. (1995). The first two years of school: Teacher-child relationships and deflections in children's classroom adjustment. *Development and Psychopathology, 7*, 295–312. doi:10.1017/S0954579400006519

Pullis, M. (1985). Student's temperament characteristics and their impact on decisions by resource and mainstream teachers. *Learning Disability Quarterly, 8*, 109–122.

Rudasill, K. M., Gallagher, K. C., & White, J. M. (2010). Temperamental attention and activity, classroom emotional support, and academic achievement in third grade. *Journal of School Psychology, 48*(2), 113–134. doi:10.1016/j.jsp.2009.11.002

Rudasill, K. M., Reio, T. G., Stipanovic, N., & Taylor, J. E. (2010). A longitudinal study of student-teacher relationship quality, difficult temperament, and risky behavior from childhood to early adolescence. *Journal of School Psychology, 48*, 389–412. doi:10.1016/j.jsp.2010.05.001

Sutherland, K. S. (2000). Promoting positive interactions between teachers and students with emotional/behavioral disorders. *Preventing School Failure, 44*(3), 110–115. doi:10.1080/10459880009599792

Tamis-LeMonda, C. S., Briggs, R. D., McClowry, S. G., & Snow, D. (2008). Challenges to the study of African American parenting: Conceptualization, sampling, research approaches, measurement, and design. *Parenting: Science & Practice, 8*(4), 319–358. doi:10.1080/15295190802612599

Yoon, J. S. (2002). Teacher characteristics as predictors of teacher-student relationships: Stress, negative affect, and self efficacy. *Social Behavior & Personality: An International Journal, 30*(5), 485–493.

PART II

THE 2 Ss OF TEMPERAMENT-BASED CLASSROOM MANAGEMENT— SCAFFOLDING AND STRETCHING

PART I of this book focused on the 3 Rs of temperament-based classroom management: Recognize, Reframe, and Respond. The 2 Ss, Scaffolding and Stretching, are presented in this part II. Scaffolding and stretching are teacher strategies that work interactively to support children's development.

Children come to school to learn! Much of what children learn in school happens, not in isolation, but within social interactions. As elegantly explained by Lev Semenovich Vygotsky (1962; 1978), learning occurs in a child's zone of proximal development (ZPD) when an adult or a more advanced classmate supports, or scaffolds, the learner. Learning in the ZPD, at first, occurs only within the dyadic interaction. With adequate scaffolding, however, the learning becomes internalized by the child. Gradually, the child decreases the need for support and gains independent mastery.

Scaffolding, in the education field, is usually applied to cognition. The tenets of scaffolding, however, also are applicable to students' social-emotional development. In chapter 4, teacher strategies for scaffolding students are discussed. By preparing and maintaining a positive classroom environment, teachers scaffold their students.

Stretching is the second S of temperament-based classroom management. As will be explained it chapter 5, stretching is deliberate teacher actions intended to foster the self-regulation of children in temperamentally challenging situations. Chapter 6 discusses how the social competence of students can also be stretched.

REFERENCES

Vygotsky, L. S. (1962). *An experimental study of concept formation.* Cambridge, MA: MIT Press.
Vygotsky, L. S. (1978). *Mind in society: The development of higher psychological processes.* Cambridge, MA: MIT Press.

CHAPTER 4

PREPARING AND MAINTAINING A POSITIVE CLASSROOM ENVIRONMENT

AHHHH, it's August! Teachers in most school districts in the United States are sensing the end of summer and the impending start of another school year. The annual countdown begins. Depending on where the teachers live, they may be tallying the number of days left to sun on the beach, enjoying leisurely dinners, or engaging in midmorning trips to the mall before the school year begins. Probably the teachers are also strategizing on how to provide their new students with a positive classroom environment.

IN THIS CHAPTER:

- Strategies for preparing the classroom before the school year begins are presented.

- Suggestions for engaging students in maintaining the classroom environment during the early weeks of the school year are offered.

- The importance of teacher monitoring and remaining consistent is discussed as applicable throughout the school year.

- Procedures are presented for dealing with student noncompliance and disruptive behavior.

- A checklist of evidence-based yet practical strategies for preparing and maintaining a positive classroom environment is provided.

A number of resources in print and on the Internet offer teachers suggestions on planning and maintaining a positive classroom environment. Many of the recommended practices, however, lack evidence that they work (Simonsen, Fairbanks, Briesch, Myers, & Sugai, 2008). Research studies have explicated strategies that are effective. Many of those strategies are presented in this chapter and summarized in a checklist at the end of the chapter.

Positive classroom environments are designed to support students' academic and social-emotional development. Skilled teachers use a number of effective strategies to scaffold their students, thereby assuring that the classroom is positive for everyone.

Before the school year begins, skilled teachers deliberately plan their classrooms to reflect their teaching philosophy and classroom management principles. Then in the early weeks of the school year, the teachers make classroom procedures explicit to the students and engage them in activities that will help them scaffold each other. Throughout the school year, the teachers monitor their students and are consistent in their disciplinary procedures in order to maintain a positive classroom environment. Individual students who are noncompliant or disruptive especially require scaffolding from their teacher and peers until they can gain mastery of their own behavior.

ICON 4.1.
Scaffolding Students

Scaffolding, from a temperament perspective, occurs when an adult or a more advanced classmate supports a child during a temperamentally challenging situation.

BEFORE THE SCHOOL YEAR BEGINS

Preparing a safe and warm environment. The way that a classroom is prepared sends a powerful message to students on the first day of school. A classroom that is welcoming sets the tone for the entire school year. It tells the students that the teacher readied the classroom so that they can immediately engage in the business and joy of learning.

How students perceive their classrooms and school has been the subject of many focus groups (Maxwell, 2000). Students are cognizant of their school's physical environment. They enthusiastically assert that a clean, well-maintained school is important to them. A safe and welcoming classroom and school provides them a sense of security and pride. Students particularly react to the esthetics of their classrooms. They appreciate colorful and grade-appropriate visual displays. Care, however, should be taken so that the physical environment is not so overstimulating that it becomes a distraction (Ahrentzen & Evans, 1984).

Parents also need to feel welcomed. Information about the upcoming year and the classroom procedures should be made available to them. Parents also appreciate knowing classroom and school visitation policies and teacher expectations regarding their involvement.

Strategizing on the physical layout of the classroom. Few teachers have the luxury of having all the space, furniture, and instructional materials they would like. Instead teachers have to make decisions that maximize and organize their available resources. Each decision has implications on how independently the students will be able to function. Encouraging the children to be self-reliant is advantageous for the students and their teachers. When students are independently engaged in their activities, teachers have more time to work with individuals or groups of students. They also spend less time managing their students' behavior at the expense of instructional time.

Procedures need to be devised to make the classroom optimally functional for the students. Specific locations can be devoted to various functions such as the library area or choice centers. Visualizing traffic patterns can help assess how students will be able to access the various classroom locations without disturbing other students who may be engaged in quiet activities.

In a related issue, instructional materials should be logically organized and easily accessed. A developmentally appropriate organizational system can help students keep track of their materials. Cubbies work well with younger children; folders are more appropriate for older students.

The ideal physical arrangement of a classroom allows for flexibility to accommodate a variety of instructional modalities. In general, a structured physical environment promotes better academic outcomes and less disruptive behaviors (Simonsen et al., 2008). Many preservice teachers and experienced ones, as well, are surprised to learn that arranging seats in rows results in greater student attentiveness and cognitive gains (MacAulay, 1990; Wannarka & Ruhl, 2008). Grouping boys and girls together also supports attentiveness. Disruptive students benefit the most from seating in rows (Wheldall & Lam, 1987). Other implications regarding the physical layout of the classroom are discussed in box 4.1.

The generalization that rows are better does not apply when social interactions are the focus or when there is a group assignment (Simonsen et al., 2008). As will be discussed in chapter 6, the social competency skills of students can be enhanced when children have opportunities to work with each other. When assigning group work, clustered desks or semicircles are the better choice (Wannarka & Ruhl, 2008).

Develop procedures for classroom routines. Another aspect of classroom planning involves formulating procedures for routine noninstructional activities like collecting lunch money, taking attendance, or collecting permission slips. When properly devised and used, such procedures require a minimum of instructional time and little direct teacher involvement. Likewise, routines can be developed so that students can efficiently and independently handle relocating furniture and supplies for various class functions.

Other classroom procedures reflect a teacher's expectations for student behavior. Careful forethought is necessary to identify the behaviors that a teacher deliberately

BOX 4.1. AN FYI: LOCATION, LOCATION, LOCATION!

The placement of furniture and materials makes a difference in student behavior, as the following experiment demonstrates. Students with moderate learning difficulties and disruptive classroom behavior were observed after the physical layout of their classroom was changed four times (Wheldall & Lam, 1987). The students were first seated around tables, then in rows, followed by tables and, again, in rows. Disruption was three times higher when the students were seated at tables. On-task behavior doubled when the students were in rows. The teachers were also affected by the changes in seating arrangements. Teachers provided more positive and less negative feedback when the students were seated in rows.

Other studies show how even small-scale changes in the physical arrangement of a classroom make a difference in students' selection of curricular materials and choice of activities. Weinstein (1977) successfully restructured a third grade classroom and increased students' use of various curricular materials by installing shelves and attractively organizing the materials on them so that they were more accessible to the students. As a result, students increased their use of sections of the classroom that they had previously avoided. Likewise, after reconstructing a distinct library area in a quiet corner of the classroom and increasing the variety of available resources, students' independent use of reading materials increased (Morrow & Weinstein, 1982).

The physical arrangement of the classroom also makes a difference in how students interact with each other (Morrow & Weinstein, 1982; Weinstein, 1977). Granström (1996) found that 90 percent of students' interactions occurred among children who sat close to each other; 68 percent of the student exchanges were between children sitting next to each other. And in what will be no surprise to teachers, more student interactions occurred in the back of the room than in the front.

The classroom environment can be enriched by taking into account that students have a variety of temperaments. Children are niche-pickers (Scarr, 1992; Strelau, 2008): they gravitate toward places that provide them with a comfortable level of stimulation. Goodness of fit can be enhanced by arranging the classroom so that there are some quiet nooks, with other designated areas for activities that are more energetic or social.

Another example of how students are niche-pickers was identified by Weinstein (1977). She found that use of study carrels by boys was related to their temperament. Those who were highly sociable seldom requested to work in study booths. Boys who were highly distractible or who were aggressive, however, were more likely to prefer study carrels so that they could more easily concentrate on their work.

encourages. Based on their own values and attitudes, teachers, like parents, differ to some degree in the behaviors that they regard favorably or not (i.e., those that are tolerated versus others that they deem unacceptable). In other words, what is acceptable or even encouraged behavior in one classroom may not be tolerated by another teacher. For example, some teachers are much more tolerant of students enthusiastically calling out answers to questions. Other teachers prefer that students raise their hands and respond only after they have been called upon. Neither way is "correct." Both ways, however, will have implications for how the classroom functions on a daily basis (and its energy and noise level!).

ENGAGING THE STUDENTS DURING THE EARLY WEEKS OF THE SCHOOL YEAR

During the early weeks of the school year, skilled teachers give students opportunities to practice the classroom procedures they devised before the school year began (Colvin, Sugai, Good, & Lee, 1997). When the children meet their behavioral expectations by following the procedures, the teachers provide positive feedback. When the procedures are not followed, the teachers give a reminder with a clear corrective instruction. As a result, students quickly become accustomed to classroom procedures and routines. Transitions between activities become predictable and are efficiently handled with minimal loss of classroom instructional time (Kern & Clemens, 2007). The early-year organizational strategizing and practicing pays off. As the year progresses, students in well-organized classrooms are more independent and only require occasional reminders to follow the classroom routines (Kern & Clemens, 2007).

In the classroom of the less-skilled teachers, the lack of preparation at the beginning of the year has negative and cumulative consequences. Student classroom disruptive behavior increases during the year and diverts time from instruction (Cameron, Connor, & Morrison, 2005). In reaction to their students' misbehavior, less-skilled teachers react harshly and fail to state clear directives for better behavior. Transitions in their classrooms are particularly time consuming and fraught with disruptive student behavior. The teachers continue to devote time to procedural instructions between activities throughout the year. As a result, the students remain dependent on their teachers for guidance about their schedule and the procedures that should instead be automatic.

Conducting classroom meetings in the early weeks of the school year is a great way to engage students in making explicit classroom behavioral expectations. By identifying appropriate classroom behaviors together, students participate in a group buy-in. The process provides a mechanism for students to scaffold each other's behavior.

Although the underlying goals of the classroom meetings are the same regardless of the age of the students, the dialogue can be adjusted to match the children's vocabulary. For example, a developmentally appropriate term primary grade students typically use for behavioral expectations is "classroom rules." For older students, "classroom community principles" is a better phrase.

BOX 4.2. ENGAGING SECONDARY GRADE STUDENTS IN IDENTIFYING THE CLASSROOM PRINCIPLES

Classroom Meeting #1

Sometime during the first week of the school year, hold a class meeting with your students to identify the rules that they think everyone in their classroom should follow. Tell the students that a discussion about the consequences of not following the rules will be the focus of another meeting. Begin the discussion by asking the students to identify what gives them a sense of belonging and responsibility in their classroom. Then using a t-diagram, like the one that follows, ask the students to nominate rules and then to identify a behavior associated with each one. Encourage your students to think positively:

What's the rule?	What does it look like?

Classroom Meeting #2

In a second class meeting, ask the students to color-code their rules into categories. Then have the students finalize their rules so that they have no more than five positively worded statements. Transfer the rules onto a poster board and place it visibly in the classroom. Copy the rules onto a portable version like the one included in figure 4.1. Send two copies of the portable version home with the children with a note requesting that the children's parents speak with them about the classroom principles. Ask the parents to sign one of the copies and return it to school with their child.

Identifying the classroom rules/principles is likely to require two meetings. The first is for brainstorming ideas. A second meeting will be necessary to distill the students' broad ideas into specific rules or principles with examples that specify specific actions. Box 4.2 provides guidelines for conducting meetings #1 and #2 with secondary grade students. The guidelines can easily be adapted for primary grade students.

An example of a set of rules for kindergarten students and classroom principles for fifth graders is below.

An Example of Our Classroom Rules for Kindergarten Students

1. Be nice
   - Be kind to your classmates
   - Take turns
   - Raise your hand when you want to answer a question

2. Do your work
3. Be safe
   - Keep your hands and feet to yourself
   - Listen to directions

An Example of Our Classroom Principles for Fifth Grade Students

1. Be respectful
   - Raise your hand to speak
   - Listen to others when they speak
   - Respect school property
2. Do your best
   - Pay attention in class
   - Turn in your work on time
3. Be responsible
   - Come to class on time
   - Bring your books and supplies

After the rules or principles are agreed upon, they should be posted in the classroom so that everyone can easily see them. A portable version like the one shown in figure 4.1 can be sent home with the students. Parents can be asked to speak with their students about the list and to sign the copy acknowledging that they have done so.

Although organizing a classroom prior to the start of the school year is critical, alterations may be warranted after observing actual student traffic and usage at the various centers. The students can be engaged in problem-solving the situation in another classroom meeting. After the alterations are made, the students can assess if their solution worked or whether it needs to be tweaked.

THROUGHOUT THE SCHOOL YEAR

Monitoring. Some teacher strategies, like monitoring and being consistent, are applicable throughout the school year. Classrooms are busy places. Yet, remarkably, skilled teachers monitor each of their students as well as the collective group. In his classic study of classroom management, Kounin (1970) coined the term "withitness" to describe teachers who are aware of what is going on all over their classroom. Teachers who are high in withitness handle small behavior problems before they escalate. They also can accurately identify who is misbehaving or initiating a negative interaction.

The physical presence of the teacher makes a difference in students' classroom behavior. Fifer (1986) observed that when teachers are in the front of the classroom, the students in the back are more disruptive. If, however, the teacher walks around the class, student behavior improves.

Additional insight into what is going on in the classroom occurs when a temperament lens is applied. Students with high task persistence are likely to derive pleasure

Our Classroom Community Principles

1. _____

   _____

2. _____

   _____

3. _____

   _____

4. _____

   _____

5. _____

   _____

Figure 4.1 Our Classroom Community Principles

from assignments that require concentration. Those who have lower attentional levels will benefit from alternative activities that cover the same content but are faster paced. A guaranteed path to student boredom, however, is an assignment that is too easy. Moderate difficulty increases engagement. Optimal engagement, or "flow," occurs when a student who is highly skilled is challenged to reach an even higher proficiency level (Shernoff & Csikszentmihalyi, 2009). In such situations, the student experiences high concentration and pleasure in the learning activity that, in turn, advances their skills to an even higher level (Shernoff & Csikszentmihalyi, 2009).

Monitoring also entails assessing changes in students' moods. Taking an achievement test or being rejected by a classmate are just two examples of circumstances that may be stressful or even overwhelming for a school-age child. When distressed, some students will exhibit disruptive behavior. Strategies for dealing with disruptive students will be explained later in this chapter.

Other students will withdraw and internalize their distress by becoming anxious or withdrawn. Teachers usually find it easier to identify disruptive behavior than internalized problems (Weeks, Coplan, & Kingsbury, 2009). An empathic teacher, however, can help children who internalize their distress to better cope with it. Box 4.3 provides suggestions on scaffolding such students.

Being consistent. In addition to monitoring, consistency is necessary for maintaining a positive classroom environment. Student compliance is enhanced when

> **BOX 4.3. SCAFFOLDING STUDENTS WHO INTERNALIZE THEIR DISTRESS**
>
> Students who internalize often are unable to volunteer why they are feeling distressed. Instead teachers can scaffold such students by inviting them to talk about their situation. When attempting to intervene, speak privately to the child and mention that you have noticed he or she seems upset lately. Ask the child whether there is something that is bothering him or her.
>
> Some children are reluctant or unable to verbalize what is upsetting them. Creative activities such as drawing or writing stories can be an effective medium for children to express themselves. Using puppets with younger children is another way that children can feel protected enough to explain what is concerning them.
>
> Oftentimes, children's worries are lessened by speaking with an adult who can help them problem-solve their concerns. Some children, however, may be dealing with serious problems that require a more concerted effort. Engaging a mental health professional who specializes in children is recommended when a student is unresponsive to a teacher's intervention.

consistency occurs. Classroom behavioral expectations and the disciplinary strategies that teachers use in response to student noncompliance or disruptive behavior should be consistent from day to day.

Consistency is also needed when there is more than one adult in the classroom. Examples of other adults might include another teacher, a teacher's aide, a student teacher, or a parent helper. Children become confused if there is inconsistency among the adults in how they manage the classroom. Some children may even take advantage of adult inconsistencies and, thereby, complicate the relationships among the adults.

The ideal time to reach agreement about classroom management is before the school year begins or prior to the introduction of another adult in the classroom. Discussion about classroom management strategies may be needed as the school year progresses if it becomes clear that inconsistencies are occurring. A meeting to resolve the differences among the adults should be scheduled when the students are not present. The first tactic will be to identify as nonjudgmentally as possible the various inconsistencies in expectations and in disciplinary strategies utilized. Then the adults should aim to reach consensus on what strategies to use to ensure better classroom management.

MAINTAINING THE CLASSROOM ENVIRONMENT BY DEALING WITH NONCOMPLIANCE AND DISRUPTIVE BEHAVIOR

Even in classrooms in which a considerable effort has been made to maintain a positive environment, it is likely that some children, at least occasionally, will exhibit behavior problems. When disruptive behavior occurs, students rely on their teacher to reestablish order within their classroom. Effective teachers apply a discipline strategy that reinforces the values and behavioral expectations previously agreed upon by the students in the class meetings. Decisive action by a teacher prevents minor disruptions from escalating into more serious behavioral problems.

Discipline is primarily symbolic. It reestablishes that the teacher is in charge of the classroom—not the disruptive student. And, importantly, discipline assists the student in understanding that a particular behavior was inappropriate. Optimal discipline also scaffolds the student to gain better self-control.

Teachers who are efficacious in managing student behavior know the right amount of control to exert. Discipline is different from punishment—which is excessive and retaliatory. To avoid punishing a noncompliant or disruptive student forethought is necessary. Responding in the "heat of a battle" is likely to be reactive and counterproductive—a situation that can easily lead to unnecessary, and often ineffective, harsh punishment. Box 4.4 lists examples of harsh punishment that should not be used.

Rather than deciding how to handle noncompliance or disruptive behavior when it unexpectedly occurs, a three-level classroom discipline plan prevents teachers from feeling caught off-guard. Like the classroom rules or principles, the ideal way to develop a discipline plan is with the students in a classroom meeting. At the very least, the discipline plan should be communicated to the students so they are aware of the three steps.

A Classroom Discipline Plan. Think of a discipline plan as a three-step ladder: a reminder, the next step, and the "big one." When dealing with misbehavior, go up the ladder only as far as necessary to gain the student's compliance. In other words, advance to the higher steps only when the lower rungs of disciplinary strategies have not been effective. The three discipline steps of appropriate management strategies are illustrated in figure 4.2.

Step 1: Use a reminder

Often, a simple reminder is all that is necessary to gain student compliance. One type of reminder is a short directive to redirect your student or to regain their attention. If your student cannot handle complex statements or has a temperament low in task persistence, make one clear request at a time. For example, "Gretchen, finish your math worksheet," as opposed to "Gretchen, do your math and then work on your history assignment."

Another type of reminder may be as simple as saying the student's name with a particular type of inflection, raising your eyebrow, or expressing surprise regarding the student's behavior: "Jacob! That just isn't like you."

Your communication style will greatly contribute to your success in redirecting the behavior of your students with a reminder. An irritable response, which is counterproductive, indicates that you are not in control of the situation. Instead calmly and deliberately use *adequate* statements when giving a reminder. Deliver a verbal reminder decisively and with good voice control.

BOX 4.4. AVOIDING HARSH PUNISHMENT

An important distinction exists between discipline that teaches a child about appropriate behavior and harsh punishment. Appropriate disciplinary strategies match the child's development level to the seriousness of the infraction. Ironically, teachers who perceive themselves as not having the power to control their students' behavior use more force than necessary (Bugental, Lewis, Lin, Lyon, & Kopeikin, 1999). Harsh punishment that is excessive makes the child feel ashamed. In response to harsh punishment, a student may also retaliate against the teacher or act even more aggressively with peers.

Examples of harsh punishments that should not be used are listed below:

- Canceling an important event: a planned field trip, a classroom party, or the celebration of the student's birthday in class.
- Denying your student lunch or a treat when the rest of the class is receiving one.
- Refusing to let the student participate in gym or recess. This tactic is not only harsh but is counterproductive for children whose temperament is high in activity. Gym class and recess allow a child to expend excess energy, which may, in turn, help the student be more focused and less fidgety during class time.
- Yelling or embarrassing the child, especially in front of classmates or other people. Ridiculing a student in this way is likely to leave the child feeling resentful. The student may also learn that such harsh behavior is acceptable if one is upset or angry.
- Punishing the children for an extended length of time. A child's behavior might after an infraction be exemplary (or at least, commendable), but he or she is essentially in "debtor's prison," without a way to rectify the situation.
- Using any kind of physical punishment.

Almost all teachers make occasional mistakes when disciplining their students. If as an afterthought, you realize that you have inadvertently used a harsh punishment, first give yourself time to regain your composure. Then discuss with your student that after careful reconsideration, you have decided that a lesser consequence will suffice for the misbehavior.

Signals are a particular type of reminder and can be directed to the whole class or to an individual student. A whole-class signal can be an effective way to get the students' attention when the classroom has gotten too noisy or when you want to transition to another activity. If you are going to use a classroom signal, use the same one consistently so that your students immediately recognize it. Examples of classroom signals are turning off the classroom lights, singing a short chorus, or clapping your hands with a particular rhythm.

When you use a classroom signal, pause to give the class a chance to respond. If the majority of the class has not responded after three seconds, then acknowledge

The Reminder

Give the student one reminder or use a pre-negotiated signal. If your student does not comply, go to The Next Step.

Examples:
- A raised eyebrow
- Saying the student's name in a firm voice
- A pre-negotiated signal

The Next Step

The next step includes your usual classroom management strategy. If your student does not comply, go to The Big One.

Examples:
- Loss of a privilege (such as waiting until the other students have chosen their choice time activity).
- Losing one's turn at a classroom responsibility (such as line leader or paper monitor).
- Time-out for a few minutes in a quiet area of the classroom.
- Sending the student to another classroom for a few minutes.
- Contact with the child's parents.

The Big One

The Big One tells your student that the misbehavior will not be tolerated in your classroom. The Big One should be used only in instances in which the student refuses to comply.

Examples:
- Referral to the school's guidance counselor.
- Referral to the school's psychologist.
- Sending the child to the principal's office.

Figure 4.2 Three-Step Classroom Discipline Ladder

some of the children who have responded: "I notice that Felicity is ready for our history class. So are Henry and Carl." Be sure to recognize the students who tend to be less compliant. They really need your acknowledgment of their good behavior.

Another type of signal is effective with an individual student who repeatedly has difficulty complying with your requests. Individual signals are an effective and powerful communication tool between a teacher and a student (McAuliffe, Hubbard, & Romano, 2009). Importantly, individual signals should be private; no one else in the room needs to witness the interaction. Younger children like to call them a "secret signal."

To implement a signal with a student, first discuss the need for the signal. Then ask the student for suggestions in selecting a signal. An example of a negotiation with a student on the selection of a signal is in box 4.5. If you decide to use a nonverbal signal, be sure that you have your student's attention before you deliver it. Whether the signal is nonverbal or verbal, maintain eye contact with the student until he or she acknowledges having received the signal.

BOX 4.5. AGREEING ON AN INDIVIDUAL SIGNAL WITH A STUDENT

Ms. Jennings: Hey, Freddy! I've noticed that you really enjoy interacting with your friends when we're working on group projects. But you seem to have difficulty when you are supposed to focus on your independent assignments and often distract the children who are sitting around you. Maybe I can help you to focus better. I have an idea. Would you like to hear about it?

Freddy: Sure.

Ms. Jennings: What if I give you a signal to remind you to get back to work?

Freddy: How would that work?

Ms. Jennings: Well, we make up a signal that only you and I understand—something like tapping once on the end of your desk or perhaps pulling on my left earring.

Freddy: Oh, I like pulling on your earring better. Nobody else will know what that means.

Ms. Jennings: OK, so when I notice that you are distracting the other kids, I'll pull on my left earring. What will that signal to you, Freddy?

Freddy: It will say, "Get back to work, Freddy! And leave your friends alone."

Ms. Jennings: Exactly!

A reminder should be used only once in response to an episode of noncompliance. Repeating the reminder diminishes the likelihood that it will be effective in subsequent uses. If the misbehavior is not curtailed by a reminder, then apply a management strategy from Step 2.

Step 2: Your usual classroom management strategy

Reminders don't always work. When they do not, advance to Step 2 in your disciplinary ladder. Compliance with the management strategies for Step 2 is enhanced when students are engaged in the process of deciding how misbehavior will be handled in their classroom. Although the ultimate responsibility for selecting discipline strategies for Step 2 resides with the teacher, input from the students is valuable. Box 4.6 includes suggestions for conducting another classroom meeting to discuss classroom management strategies that will follow noncompliance or disruptive behavior.

An excellent disciplinary strategy for school-age children who have not responded to a reminder is the loss of a privilege. Surprisingly, the lost privilege can be a minor one and still be effective. Examples of appropriate lost privileges include waiting until the other students have chosen their choice time activity or losing one's turn to have a desired classroom responsibility like being the line leader or paper monitor.

Time-out can be another effective classroom consequence for a student whose behavior has been disruptive. If you are going to use it as a disciplinary strategy, pick a quiet, safe place for it in your classroom. While in time-out, the student should be removed from attractive distractions. Use the same place consistently so that your students knows what you mean when you say, "Go to the time-out place for six minutes."

The appropriate length of time for time-out is related to your student's age—one minute per year is the right amount. For example, time-out for a first grade student should only be six minutes long. A disciplinary strategy that goes on for an extended length of time ceases to be effective because school-age children have a limited understanding of time. After a brief period of time, the child will have forgotten why he or she was placed in time-out, thereby undermining its purpose. Using a timer helps your student understand the length of time for the time-out and is likely to diminish the struggle between the two of you regarding the completion of the time-out.

BOX 4.6. A CLASSROOM MEETING TO DISCUSS THE USUAL CLASSROOM MANAGEMENT STRATEGY

Another classroom meeting can be devoted to discussing the consequences of not following the classroom rules or principles. Explain to the students that you are implementing a three-step discipline plan. Encourage them to offer suggestions for the class signal. Then after selecting one, be prepared to discuss various appropriate strategies that might be used when individual students do not respond to a reminder. Select one strategy that will usually be used in the classroom and one that is more appropriate for activities outside the classroom such as field trips or when walking in the halls. Communicating about your preplanned Step 2 discipline strategies is advantageous to you and your students because it eliminates the need for negotiating during what is likely to be an emotionally charged incident.

Calmly set the timer and tell your student to return to the classroom activities when the bell rings. Remember that once the student has completed time-out, the incident is over. Do not lecture or nag the child about whatever occurred that led to the time-out.

Another effective classroom disciplinary strategy is to allow the *natural consequences* of the misbehavior to occur. For example, suppose you tell the class that they can start their homework as soon as they complete the assignment they have been given. Many of the students work diligently and finish their homework while at school. The natural consequences are that the students who did not use their time well will have homework to complete that evening. Letting natural consequences occur can be a very powerful management strategy, but a teacher must always use good judgment when using it. Sometimes the natural consequences can be devastating to a student because it results in harsh punishment.

Another type of consequence for misbehavior is to assign a task to the student that makes amends by benefiting the classroom. Examples include alphabetizing the books in the classroom library or reorganizing a section of the classroom. When possible, engage the student in selecting the task, but be sure that the student does not select too difficult an assignment.

Step 3: The Big One

On those, hopefully, rare instances when a student's problem behavior has not been rectified by completing Step 2, advance to Step 3: "The Big One." The Big One should be reserved for students whose behavior is frequently noncompliant or involves a very serious infraction. Such behavior can be stressful for a teacher whose efforts to contain it have been unsuccessful.

Frequently, Step 3 discipline strategies engage other school personnel such as the principal or school counselor. Individual schools and school districts often have policies on how to deal with behavior problems that cannot be effectively resolved by the classroom teacher. Be sure to know your school and district policy for student misbehavior that does not resolve with your teacher strategies.

Using a temperament lens when applying disciplinary strategies. Children respond differently to classroom management strategies. Temperament helps to explain why. Although a three-step discipline plan is an asset for classroom management, using a temperament framework can help you modify how you apply the strategies, as explained in box 4.7.

SUMMARY

This chapter presents teachers with many practical yet effective strategies for preparing and maintaining a positive classroom environment. With adequate forethought, a classroom environment can scaffold students, thereby enhancing their academic and social-emotional development. Before the school year begins, effective teachers prepare their classroom so students are welcomed into a safe and warm environment.

BOX 4.7. MODIFYING YOUR DISCIPLINE STRATEGIES TO MATCH YOUR STUDENT'S TEMPERAMENT

Using a temperament framework can assist teachers in understanding how to modify their discipline strategies. To be most effective, reminders can be adjusted to match a student's temperament. For example, what may appear to be an appropriately firm directive for a child like Gregory the Grumpy might be intimidating to Coretta the Cautious. Children who have a tendency to withdraw, like Coretta the Cautious, may be intimidated if they perceive that their teacher's voice is harsh. In fact, they may become even more reticent to be engaged at school. A very gentle comment like "Coretta, that's enough" may be all that is needed.

While a mild reprimand is likely to be effective with Coretta the Cautious, it may not even register with Gregory the Grumpy, who requires a more definitive communication. Children who are high in negative reactivity, like Gregory the Grumpy, have particular difficulty complying with teacher directives. Their intense and negative reaction to "life happens" situations can easily predominate and bring other classroom activities to a halt. If allowed, children who are high in negative reactivity can take control of a situation and become the one who is effectively in charge of the classroom. Such misbehavior should not in any way be blamed on the child's temperament. Instead, it begins with an expression of negative reactivity that is allowed to escalate into problem behavior that requires correction. Although children who are high in negative reactivity, like Gregory the Grumpy, may be the most prone to engage in recurrent disruptive behaviors, any child can become consistently noncompliant if limits are not explicitly stated and effectively applied.

The use of a time-out also has temperament implications that explain why it does not work for all students. Some high maintenance children cannot settle down while in time-out. Instead they only get more upset. Many social/eager to try children adapt so quickly that they actually enjoy time-out! And some low task persistence children use time-out as an escape from whatever else they were supposed to do.

Having a flexible layout is conducive for engaging students in different teaching modalities. The physical layout of the classroom should maximize the students' ability to use the various resources and locations without distracting other students. In general, highly structured classrooms foster student attentiveness and reduce disruptive behavior. Cluster desks or semicircles, however, support social interactions and group assignments.

Classroom procedures also require strategizing by teachers. Plans to routinize noninstructional activities can foster independence among the children and leave more time for teaching. Teachers also need to think about their behavioral expectations for the students.

In the early weeks of the school year, effective teachers provide students with opportunities to practice the procedures they devised so that they become routine. Student input during class meetings is used to make explicit classroom rules or procedures. So are the consequences for student noncompliance or disruptive behavior.

Throughout the year, monitoring and consistency are needed to maintain a positive classroom environment. Although many classroom activities and interactions occur simultaneously, effective teachers monitor the students individually and collectively, a term that Kounin (1970) calls "withitness."

Consistency in the strategies that teachers and other adults in the classroom use in response to student noncompliance or disruptive behavior is also important. Preplanning a three-step discipline ladder is recommended. Step 1 is a verbal or nonverbal reminder. Classroom signals or individually negotiated secret signals are other types of reminders. Examples of Step 2 strategies include a loss of privilege, time-out, or allowing the natural consequences of the misbehavior to occur. Step 3, reserved for students who are frequently noncompliant or disruptive, often involves other school personnel. Using a temperament framework can provide insight into how teacher strategies may need to be modified for optimal use.

A checklist summarizing these strategies and others is posted in appendix A at the end of this chapter. The next chapter focuses on stretching strategies that can enhance student self-regulation. Instructions on how to develop and implement a Cooperation Contract for students who exhibit a repetitive behavior problem will also be presented.

CLASS DISCUSSION

- Design a schematic model of a classroom. Prepare to discuss your rationale for your classroom design.
- Plan a classroom routine that demonstrates how physical movement will occur in your classroom when lining up for lunchtime or moving to choice centers. Role-play practicing the routine with your colleagues acting as elementary school students.
- Create a classroom display that welcomes the students at the beginning of the year. Explain how you will transition your display into an exhibition of student work.
- Role-play one of the classroom meetings that were discussed in this chapter. First conduct the meeting with primary grade children and then role-play another one with older students.

OPTIONAL CASE STUDY ASSIGNMENT

If "Student C"'s teacher is agreeable, negotiate an individual signal with Student C. Observe the student's response when the signal is used.

APPENDIX A: CHECKLIST FOR PREPARING AND MAINTAINING YOUR CLASSROOM

Before the school year begins

Prepare a safe and warm environment—
- Assure that procedures are in place so that only people who are safe enter the school and your classroom.
- Prepare classroom and school displays that welcome the students to the new school year.
- Prepare information about the school and your classroom for your students' parents. Explain your visiting policies to the parents.

Strategize on how to arrange the physical layout of your classroom space—
- Arrange the furniture so that there is an adequate space for the students to move with ease into the various locations like the library area, restroom, or choice centers.
- Arrange the classroom so that student traffic does not go through designated work areas. Think about using *signposts* (such as arrows) to communicate directions.
- Avoid placing too many learning materials near the exit, the sink, or the meeting areas.
- Place your reading area away from the more interactive learning centers.
- Plan designated areas for students who desire a quiet environment and for those who prefer more social interactions.
- Plan to have students do messy work where the "mess" will not interfere with other student activities.
- Be sure that you are able to monitor your students from everywhere in the room and that your students can see you.
- Plan adequate space and storage for students' personal belongings and for receiving notes and other materials from their parents.
- Clearly label all materials and their storage compartments. Color-code when possible and use child-friendly language, pictures, and/or illustrations.
- Cubbies or mailboxes are recommended for younger students and folders are suggested for older students.
- Consider using color-coded storage areas. For example: things in *red* compartments stay at school; things in *blue* compartments go home.

Plan the seating arrangement of your students—
- Assure that there is enough "elbow room" for students when engaged in table work or for class meetings.
- Alternate boys and girls in your arrangements.
- Place students with disruptive behavior near the front of the room.
- Use rows for times when you want student attention to be directed at you.
- Prepare an alternative room arrangement for times when you would like students to work together.

- Plan classroom procedures and routine:
  - Think about how the children will move furniture (like their chairs) for the various class functions.
  - Decide how often and under what circumstances you will allow students to enter and exit the classroom.
  - Plan procedures for noninstructional activities such as collecting lunch money, taking attendance, or collecting permission slips. Establish routines so that the students handle such matters independently and unobtrusively.

During the early weeks of the school year
- Practice class and school procedures with the students.
- Conduct class meetings with the students to establish class rules or procedures.
- Provide positive and clear corrective feedback regarding students' performance in carrying out organizational activities.
- Replace the displays that you made for the beginning of the school year with student work.

Throughout the school year
- Monitor the behavior of the students. Provide positive feedback when their behavior is appropriate.
- Prepare instructional materials and supplies prior to the students' arrival each day.
- Label and store materials that are intended for your students to use at their eye level.
- Place materials that you *do not* want the children to use in areas that are not accessible to them.
- Avoid clutter. A clean and organized room sets a good example for your students regarding their own desks and schoolwork.
- Post a developmentally appropriate daily and weekly schedule so that the students know what to expect.
- Observe how students are using the various portions of your classroom. If a change in the room arrangement needs to be made, discuss the reason with the students. Involve the students in planning the changes and in identifying potential stumbling blocks.
- Be consistent in the strategies you and other adults in the classroom use in response to student noncompliance or disruptive behavior.
- Engage the students in developing a three-step discipline plan:
  - Step 1: Use a reminder
  - Step 2: Usual classroom management strategy
  - Step 3: The big one, which usually involves other school personnel
- Adjust your management strategies so that they match your students' temperaments.

RECOMMENDED READINGS

Bugental, D. B., Lewis, J. C., Lin, E., Lyon, J., & Kopeikin, H. (1999). In charge but not in control: The management of teaching relationships by adults with low perceived power. *Developmental Psychology, 35*, 1367–1378. doi:0.1037//0012-1649.35.6.1367

Colvin, G., Sugai, G., Good, R. H., & Lee, Y. Y. (1997). Using active supervision and pre-correction to improve transition behaviors in an elementary school. *School Psychology Quarterly. Special Issue: Changing Teacher and Staff Behavior to Benefit Children, 12*(4), 344–363. doi:10.1037/h0088967

MacAulay, D. J. (1990). Classroom environment: A literature review. *Educational Psychology, 10*(3), 239–253. doi:10.1080/0144341900100305

REFERENCES

Ahrentzen, S., & Evans, G. W. (1984). Distraction, privacy, and classroom design. *Environment and Behavior, 16*(4), 437–454. doi:10.1177/0013916584164002

Bugental, D. B., Lewis, J. C., Lin, E., Lyon, J., & Kopeikin, H. (1999). In charge but not in control: The management of teaching relationships by adults with low perceived power. *Developmental Psychology, 35*, 1367–1378. doi:10.1037/0012-1649.35.6.1367

Cameron, C. E., Connor, C. M., Morrison, F. J. (2005). Effects of variation in teacher organization on classroom functioning. *Journal of School Psychology, 43*, 61–85. doi:2080/10.1016/j.jsp.2004.12.002

Colvin, G., Sugai, G., Good, R. H., & Lee, Y. Y. (1997). Using active supervision and pre-correction to improve transition behaviors in an elementary school. *School Psychology Quarterly. Special Issue: Changing Teacher and Staff Behavior to Benefit Children, 12*(4), 344–363. doi:10.1037/h0088967

Fifer, F. L. (1986). Effective classroom management. *Academic Therapy, 21*(4), 401–410. doi:10.1177/105345128602100402

Granström, K. (1996). Private communication between students in the classroom in relation to different classroom features. *Educational Psychology, 16*(4), 349–364. doi:10.1080/0144341960160401

Kern, L., & Clemens, N. H. (2007). Antecedent strategies to promote appropriate classroom behavior. *Psychology in the Schools. Special Issue: The Practitioner's Edition on Promoting Behavioral Competence, 44*, 65–75. doi:10.1002/pits.20206

Kounin, J. S. (1970). *Discipline and group management in classrooms.* New York, NY: Holt, Rinehart and Winston.

MacAulay, D. J. (1990). Classroom environment: A literature review. *Educational Psychology, 10*(3), 239–253. doi:10.1080/0144341900100305

Maxwell, L. E. (2000). A safe and welcoming school: What students, teachers, and parents think. *Journal of Architectural and Planning Research, 17*(4), 271–282. doi:2002-10516-001

McAuliffe, M. D., Hubbard, J. A., & Romano, L. J. (2009). The role of teacher cognition and behavior in children's peer relations. *Journal of Abnormal Child Psychology, 37*(5), 665–677. doi:http://dx.doi.org/10.1007/s10802-009-9305-5

Morrow, L. M., & Weinstein, C. S. (1982). Increasing children's use of literature through program and physical design changes. *Elementary School Journal, 83*(2), 131–137. doi:10.1086/461301

Scarr, S. (1992). Developmental theories for the 1990s: Developmental and individual differences. *Child Development, 63*, 1–19. doi:10.1111/j.1467-8624.1992.tb03591.x

Shernoff, D. J., & Csikszentmihalyi, M. (2009). Flow in schools: Cultivating engaged learners and optimal learning environments. In R. Gilman, E. S. Huebner, & M. J. Furlong (Eds.), *Handbook of positive psychology in schools* (pp. 131–145). New York, NY: Routledge/Taylor & Francis Group.

Simonsen, B., Fairbanks, S., Briesch, A., Myers, D., & Sugai, G. (2008). Evidence-based practices in classroom management: Considerations for research to practice. *Education & Treatment of Children, 31*(3), 351–380. doi:10.1353/etc.0.0007

Strelau, J. (2008). *Temperament as a regulator of behavior: After fifty years of research*. Clinton Corners, NY: Eliot Werner.

Wannarka, R., & Ruhl, K. (2008). Seating arrangements that promote positive academic and behavioural outcomes: A review of empirical research. *Support for Learning, 23*(2), 89–93. doi:10.1111/j.1467-9604.2008.00375.x

Weeks, M., Coplan, R. J., & Kingsbury, A. (2009). The correlates and consequences of early appearing social anxiety in young children. *Journal of Anxiety Disorders, 23*, 965–972. doi:10.1016/j.janxdis.2009.06.006

Weinstein, C. S. (1977). Modifying student behavior in an open classroom through changes in the physical design. *American Educational Research Journal, 14*(3), 249–262. doi:10.3102/00028312014003249

Wheldall, K., & Lam, Y. Y. (1987). Rows versus tables: II. The effects of two classroom seating arrangements on classroom disruption rate, on-task behaviour and teacher behaviour in three special school classes. *Educational Psychology, 7*(4), 303–312. doi:10.1080/0144341870070405

CHAPTER 5

ENHANCING STUDENT SELF-REGULATION

T HE ULTIMATE goal of classroom management is to enhance the ability of students to regulate their own behavior. Increasingly, educators refer to *self-regulation* as the self-adaptive processes that enable students to be successful in their academic performance as well as in their social relationships. This chapter returns to temperament theory to explicate how and why students differ in self-regulation. Temperament-based teacher strategies will be presented that will assist you in enhancing your students' self-regulation.

IN THIS CHAPTER:

- Self-regulation is defined.

- The development of self-regulation is discussed.

- Strategies that teachers can use to enhance student self-regulation are discussed.

- Guidelines for using Cooperation Contracts and their relevant applications are presented.

DEFINING SELF-REGULATION

Self-regulation is the adaptive processes that individuals use to respond appropriately to the expectations and demands of their environment. Individuals who are high in self-regulation can modulate their temperamental reactions including their emotions, attention, and motor activity (Rothbart, 2011).

Teachers easily identify the children in their classroom who are high in self-regulation. These students come to school ready and eager to learn; they pay attention in class, get along well with their teachers and peers, and adapt well to change. Children high in self-regulation are also able to set goals and create a realistic plan to achieve them. In contrast, students who are low in self-regulation are compromised in all areas of their development. Low student self-regulation is manifested in learning difficulties as well as conflictual relationships with peers, teachers, and family members (Miller, Gouley, Seifer, Dickstein, & Shields, 2004).

Importantly, children, as well as adults, differ in their capacity to self-regulate. Temperament theory explains how self-regulation develops and why some people have more self-regulation challenges than others.

THE DEVELOPMENT OF SELF-REGULATION

Self-regulation develops through the interactions that occur over time between a child's temperament and the socialization practices of parents and teachers (Rothbart, 2011). Eisenberg, Hofer, and Vaughan (2007) explain how children learn to self-regulate. For example, although babies are often frightened by unfamiliar sounds and people, the intensity of a baby's reaction is related to their temperament. Some babies are very upset by a loud noise; their crying is intense and their heart races. Other babies react less strongly; their cry is quieter and shorter in duration. These patterns extend beyond infancy and influence how children respond to their environments and interact with others. Parent responsivity (i.e., how parents care for and respond to their infant's needs) has a major impact on child development.

Infants depend on their parents for external regulation of their emotions. In response to their babies' distress, responsive parents will cuddle, talk, or try to distract their infants. These parenting strategies, intended to soothe a baby, require more parental effort if the infant's temperamental reaction is intense. Some parents become frustrated with the intense reactions of their children, especially when their efforts do not have a calming effect. Most parents, however, take delight in comforting their babies and are largely successful in their attempts to do so. Through trial and error, responsive parents learn which parenting strategies work best for their particular child (McClowry, 2003).

Babies begin to self-regulate during their first few months of life. For example, most babies calm themselves in scary or frustrating situations by sucking their thumb or looking away (Eisenberg et al., 2007). They also watch their parents for cues that suggest how they should respond. Parents who are high in self-regulation serve as good role models.

Self-regulation increases rapidly between two and seven years of age (Rothbart, 2011). Toddlers begin applying effortful control to willfully override their temperament tendencies in order to self-regulate. Effortful control is willfully inhibiting, activating, or modulating attention and behavior. It also involves planning, detecting errors, and integrating information prior to responding to a situation (Eisenberg, Smith, & Spinrad, 2011). By kindergarten, children who are high in self-regulation

Child Temperament ⟶ Child employs effortful control ⟶ Self-regulation occurs

Figure 5.1 How Self-Regulation Develops

can manage their impulses, understand other's beliefs and desires, and employ rudimentary planning and problem-solving skills (Eisenberg et al., 2007). The figure in 5.1 depicts how self-regulation develops.

Children with temperaments that are low in negative reactivity (Rothbart, 2011) and high in task persistence (Smart et al., 2003) are the most successful self-regulators. In fact, self-regulation is easy for them. Furthermore, their self-regulated behavior is advantageous at school. Because they are low in negative reactivity, these students usually get along well with their peers and their teachers. Likewise, high task persistence is an asset for the completion of assignments. A self-regulated student is also strategic in setting and achieving goals. They use problem-solving skills, time and resource management, and make revisions in their plans when necessary (Paris & Paris, 2001). In contrast, other children need to exert effortful control to override their temperament reactions in order to successfully adapt to the demands and expectations of the school environment. Teachers can help students with these temperaments expand their self-regulatory capabilities.

No matter how responsive a teacher is, classroom life will invariably present students with situations that are temperamentally challenging. Although temperamentally challenging situations cause some degree of unease for a student, they are opportunities to enhance student self-regulation. Box 5.1 illustrates examples of temperamentally challenging situations.

Enhancing a student's self-regulation requires the teacher and the child to work in tandem. As shown in figure 5.2, the teacher will scaffold the child while applying gentle stretching strategies. Think of stretching as incremental practice in overriding the child's temperamental tendencies (Denissen, van Aken, Penke, & Wood, 2013). As importantly, the student will use effortful control. Although the child's intrinsic temperament is not changed, with practice, the student may expand his or her behavioral repertoire to more successfully meet the environmental expectations.

TEACHER STRATEGIES THAT ENHANCE STUDENT SELF-REGULATION

Using a temperament lens can help teachers understand why some students experience self-regulation difficulties. For example, children who are low in task persistence are often disorganized. Those who are high in motor activity frequently have difficulty remaining seated. Children who are high in negative reactivity may express themselves in ways that upset others. Students who are high in withdrawal may quietly avoid social situations. Teacher strategies to enhance students' self-regulation include teacher talk and multicomponent behavior contracts.

BOX 5.1. HOW STUDENT SELF-REGULATION CAN BE ENHANCED THROUGH TEMPERAMENT-CHALLENGING SITUATIONS

Imagine this scenario that describes how students in Ms. Jennings's classroom, based on their temperaments, react to a multicomponent classroom project. Notice also how Ms. Jennings scaffolds the students and gently helps them stretch their self-regulatory capabilities.

Ms. Jennings's fifth grade students are engaged in a yearlong project to study the economic development of their state. The project is being conducted with fifth grade students in Mr. Morris's classroom, which is in a rural community in upstate New York. Ms. Jennings's students live in New York City. The students in the two classrooms use the Internet and other technology to organize the multifaceted project and to work collaboratively with each other. Hilary is intrigued by the project and excited to contribute. She assumes a leadership role and immediately labels file folders to organize the various components. Gregory is frustrated by the complexity of his role on the project, which is to trace the history of manufacturing in the state.

Midway through the school year, Ms. Jennings's class takes a field trip to visit the students in the rural community. Freddy is excited because he is going to meet the students who have become his "friends" through the technology tools the classrooms use. The opportunity to visit a farm as part of the day is also appealing to him. Coretta, however, is not looking forward to the day. She tells Ms. Jennings that she would prefer staying at school to research more information about her portion of the project.

Hilary and Freddy are temperamentally advantaged in this scenario. Their contributions to the project do not require that they exert a great deal of effortful control. Instead, they are energized by their experiences. Hilary enjoys organizing the vast amount of material and is likely to receive a great deal of positive feedback from her teacher and classmates about the organizational system she created. Freddy's sociability is appreciated not only by his teacher and classmates, but also by their collaborators in the rural school. By the end of the project, Freddy will have many new friends and will enthusiastically talk about farming and the other industries in which New York State is engaged.

In contrast, working on a group project with unfamiliar peers from another school is temperamentally challenging for Coretta. Likewise, completing his part of the multistep report is difficult for Gregory. In both instances, the project will require them to use a great deal of effortful control and the support of Ms. Jennings.

Teachers would be remiss in their responsibilities if they removed students from all situations that are temperamentally challenging. For example, Coretta needs to improve her social skills and Gregory would benefit greatly from building better organizational skills. If Ms. Jennings is successful in helping them stretch their temperamental tendencies, their self-regulation will be enhanced.

Ms. Jennings, however, cannot enhance her students' self-regulation by herself. Instead her students will need to exert effortful control. Because working against one's temperament requires concerted effort, it takes energy. Children arrive at school each morning with their own particular store of energy. Circumstances can reduce their energy even before the school day begins. Inadequate sleep, skipping breakfast, or family problems compromise energy stores and thereby reduce students' capacity to use effortful control to meet temperamentally challenging situations (Baumeister & Tierney, 2011).

As illustrated in the decision tree depicted in figure 5.2, students in temperamentally challenging situations can be supported by teacher strategies. The first step is to appreciate how taxing it is for a student to use effortful control to override a temperamental tendency. Stretching is serious business and should be approached judiciously. Ms. Jennings should not expect dramatic changes in her students' self-regulation.

The next step requires the teacher to assess students' self-regulation capabilities in context. Will the student be overwhelmed by the situation or can it be manageable with scaffolding and stretching? For example, Ms. Jennings will need to evaluate whether the multistep assignment is beyond Gregory's capabilities to handle independently. If so, Ms. Jennings will scaffold Gregory by helping him organize the assignment into smaller, more-manageable segments. Ms. Jennings will need to monitor Gregory's progress to make sure he doesn't become overly frustrated or fall too far behind his timeline. Additionally, Gregory will need positive feedback when he accomplishes each segment.

Ms. Jennings can use other strategies to scaffold and gently expand Coretta's self-regulation. She could ask Mr. Morris to invite one of his highly sociable students to reach out to Coretta before the field trip. Or he might ask one of Coretta's parents to accompany the class. Ms. Jennings, herself, will also need to monitor Coretta during the trip and to acknowledge her contributions to the day's events.

If stretching is unsuccessful, the student's temperamental tendency will remain the same or may even become less flexible. In addition, the student is likely to feel more anxious or frustrated and will need even more effortful control when another similar temperamentally challenging situation arises. If, however, stretching has successfully occurred, the student will have met the temperament challenge. A little less effortful control may be required the next time a similar temperamentally challenging situation arises. After multiple temperamentally challenging situations have been met, the student's self-regulation will be enhanced. Importantly, Ms. Jennings will need to be patient; growth in self-regulation occurs slowly and only with small, incremental changes.

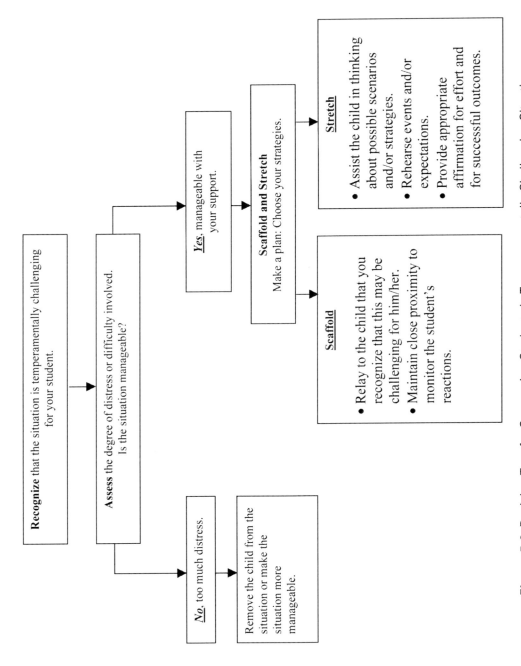

Figure 5.2 Decision Tree for Supporting Students in Temperamentally Challenging Situations

Teacher talk. One straightforward teacher strategy is using teacher talk to give temperament-sensitive verbal cues. During a classroom meeting, students can be told that everyone finds some situations challenging. For some students, thinking before they act requires effort. Those students need to use their brakes. Other students need to push themselves so that they don't get stuck. Still other students find finishing assignments challenging. They need to stay with it so they can complete their work. Most students need to take a break once in a while so they can return to their work reenergized. Table 5.1 lists child-friendly cues that scaffold and stretch a student's temperament-related behavior. When said in a neutral and quiet tone of voice, the statements cue students on how they can exert effortful control.

"Take a break" can also be used on a classroom level to enhance student self-regulation. Students perform better when they have at least a fifteen-minute recess (Barros, Silver, & Stein, 2009) and are more attentive and less fidgety after recess (Pelligrini, Huberty, & Jones, 1995).

Cooperation Contracts. A well-negotiated and well-implemented Cooperation Contract is an excellent teacher strategy for enhancing a student's self-regulation. Cooperation Contracts are applicable to a number of situations:

- Resolving a behavioral issue of a student;
- Supporting a student with attentional difficulties;
- Repairing a conflictual student-teacher relationship.

The purposes of such contracts are threefold. First, an unregulated student behavior is changed or at least reduced. Second, the teacher formalizes a way to scaffold and stretch the student's temperament-related behavior. Third, implementing a Cooperation Contract can preempt the student and teacher from engaging in a spiral of negativity.

Table 5.1. Child-Friendly Cues for Enhancing Student Self-Regulation

Relevant Temperament Dimensions	Child-Friendly Cues
High negative reactivity Low negative reactivity Low withdrawal	Use your brakes (so you can stop and think it over).
High withdrawal Low motor activity	Act when you would rather avoid doing something.
High withdrawal High negative reactivity	Shift your attention away so you don't get stuck.
Low task persistence	Stay with it so that you can finish.
High motor activity High task persistence Low task persistence	Take a break.

Cooperation Contracts are a key strategy in *INSIGHTS* (O'Connor, Cappella, McCormick, & McClowry, 2013). The foci of the contracts are remarkably commonplace. Many involve organizational issues like putting backpacks in their designated place, bringing assignments home, completing homework, and/or returning it to school the next day. Process-oriented issues include the manner in which a student speaks to their teacher, transitioning between school activities, and respecting the rights of other children by following the agreed-upon classroom rules.

Guidelines for establishing a Cooperation Contract are summarized in table 5.2. At first glance, these steps may appear deceptively simple. In reality, they require a concerted effort on your part so that the contract is successful. The satisfaction gained by resolving a behavioral issue with a student, however, can compensate for the time and effort involved.

Before you initiate a contract with a student, you need to conduct some preliminary steps. First, identify a very specific behavior that is compromising the student's development or is disruptive to the classroom community. Then analyze the components of the behavior carefully so that you can decide on one feasible goal for the contract. It is important that the student achieves the first week's goal. For example, if your student Gretchen is disorganized, choose one aspect of organization to work on during the first week. The contract goal could be disposing of half-used papers,

Table 5.2. Summary of Guidelines for Contracting with a Student

Prior to meeting with the student
1. Select one and only one reasonable goal.
2. State the goal in a positive way.
While planning the contract with the student
3. Negotiate student and teacher daily and weekly responsibilities.
4. Decide together on a daily and weekly reinforcement. (It can be a privilege or a small item.)
5. You and the student sign the contract in a business-like manner.
6. Agree on where the contract and tally sheet should be kept.
While the contract is ongoing
7. Provide no warnings.
8. Check the goal at the specified time. When achieved, place a sticker or checkmark on the tally sheet; otherwise, leave the space blank.
9. Acknowledge your student when the daily or weekly goal is met. Use optimal statements whenever possible.
10. Be sure to provide the student with the weekly reinforcement if the week's goal is met.

putting her books into her desk before dismissal, or writing down her homework assignment.

Once you have selected a goal, phrase it in a positive way. This step of the contract may sound easy but it is not for at least two reasons. Generally, by the time a teacher initiates a contract, he or she is likely to be annoyed with the student. Consequently, being positive will take a concerted effort. Some goals require a great deal of creativity in order to state positively. For example, if the goal is to get your student to stop whining, you could describe it as "speaking in a pleasant voice when asking for help" or "talking in a grown-up voice." Secondly, selecting only one goal also takes some constraint. Remember, contracts cannot be effective if they overreach.

After you have devised one positively phrased goal, begin the formal negotiation process with your student. Invite the student to join you in a quiet spot in your classroom. For example, you might speak to the student while the other children are engaged in seatwork. Set a tone for the meeting that conveys that you are taking the contract seriously. Be prepared by having a copy of the contract, a tally sheet, and something to use for your signatures. A blank contract and tally sheet are provided in figure 5.3.

Begin the negotiation process by telling the student that you notice that a particular behavior is difficult for him or her. Reassure the student that you can help him or her to develop better study habits, social skills, or whatever descriptor fits the goal by initiating a contract. Tell the student that to begin the process you have selected a goal that can be changed in a week with input from the student. Most children enjoy the contracting process and are willing to begin with the teacher's idea, especially when they realize that there are other negotiable components. If, however, your student is opposed to the goal you selected, you will need to find one that is agreeable to both of you. It is unwise to design a contract that is supposed to enhance self-regulation if the student opposes it from the start.

Once the goal is agreed upon, negotiate your respective responsibilities. For example, if the goal is to keep the student's desk neater by putting his books and supplies into the desk before the end of the day, then the student's responsibility can be to prepare his desk by 2:30 p.m. It follows that the teacher responsibility will be to check whether the goal has been accomplished at 2:45 p.m. in preparation for the 3:00 p.m. dismissal.

If the selected goal is process oriented, find a way to delimit it to a particular time, at least for the first week. For example, if the goal is to "talk in a grown-up voice," make it specific by adding "during the morning class meeting." Again, make sure that the goal is initially possible for the child. You can extend the amount of time or under what conditions in subsequent weeks.

The next item of negotiation has two parts. Determine the number of times that your student has to achieve the goal before he or she receives a weekly reinforcement. Again, it is important to be realistic so that your student can be successful. The contract should not require the student to be perfect. For example, if homework assignments are given five days a week, negotiate for three the first week. The selected reinforcement should be something small. A classroom responsibility like erasing the

Student/Teacher Cooperation Contract

Student's Name: _____

Teacher's Name: _____

> **Goal:** _____
>
> _____

Student's responsibilities: _____

_____

_____

Teacher's responsibilities: _____

_____

_____

Weekly Reinforcement: _____

_____   _____

Teacher's Signature   **Student's Signature**

Figure 5.3a Blank Student/Teacher Cooperation Contract and Tally Sheet

Cooperation Contract Tally Sheet

Student's name: _____

Goal: _____

	MONDAY	TUESDAY	WEDNESDAY	THURSDAY	FRIDAY	SATURDAY	SUNDAY
Dates: **WEEK 1**							
Dates: **WEEK 2**							
Dates: **WEEK 3**							

Figure 5.3b Continued

whiteboard or receiving something like an eraser are inexpensive but important reinforcements for students. Remember that the reinforcement is a tangible way of telling your student that you acknowledge his or her success in fulfilling the responsibilities on which you agreed. Anything more elaborate than a token object or gesture will weaken the effect of the contract because it will become the focus.

To underscore the importance of the contract, you and your student should sign it as shown in the example labeled figure 5.4. Approach the signing of the contract in a very lawyer-like way. Sit directly across from your student and have the contract and a pen (or crayon, if more developmentally appropriate) ready for the signing. Remember that if you indicate that the contract is serious, your student will respond in a like manner.

As the final step before implementing the contract, have your child assist you in placing the respective dates on the tally sheet. Then decide with the student where the contract and tally sheet should be kept. Some students will want it displayed on a bulletin board; others prefer a more private place such as in a folder on your desk.

Once the contract is in place, follow it carefully even on days when it is inconvenient. Teachers can quickly undermine the contract by failing to fulfill their part. For example, if you promised that you would check your child's backpack to see whether the appropriate materials are in it before dismissal, be sure to do so, even when the classroom activities run overtime and cause a rushed dismissal.

On days when your student has fulfilled the goal, verbally acknowledge him or her as you place a sticker on the tally sheet in the designated box. Keep in mind that if you do not have stickers, you can draw something like a smiley face or a star. Also be sure to use optimal statements whenever possible.

One way that well-intentioned teachers can undermine a Cooperation Contract is by giving the student a reminder or a warning about the agreed-upon responsibility. Because the identified responsibilities have been negotiated, reminders or warnings are counterproductive and quickly become nagging. An exception can be made for young or very forgetful students. You may need to remind them in the morning that they have a contract in place for the day.

On days when your student does not fulfill the goal, say something in a matter-of-fact voice, like "You can try again tomorrow." Do not reprimand the child. Simply leave the tally space blank. Refraining from saying anything more than a neutral statement can be difficult for some teachers, especially those who frequently engage in counterproductive responses such as nagging or lecturing.

If the goal for the week has been achieved, use the same low-key but responsive approach. Acknowledge the student's success and provide the weekly reinforcement. Then negotiate a small amendment with the student for the second week so that the responsibilities are slightly greater. For example, you may add on an additional task related to organizational skills, like putting away personal items in the clothes closet first thing in the morning. If, however, your student was unsuccessful in achieving the reinforcement, evaluate whether the goal was too ambitious. Amend the contract for another week by selecting a more obtainable goal.

Student Teacher Cooperation Contract

Student's Name: Allison McClowry

Teacher's Name: Ms. Rossi

Goal: Write down homework assignments in notebook

Child's responsibilities: Allison will write down her homework assignments in her notebook.

Teacher responsibilities: Ms. Rossi will check Allison's notebook every day at 2:15 to see whether Allison has written down all of her assignments. Allison will get a sticker if she did.

Reinforcement: Allison can select the story book on Friday if she gets at least three stickers that week.

Ms. Rossi

Teacher's Signature

Allison

Student's Signature

Figure 5.4 An Example of a Cooperation Contract

Be sure to keep the contract active and add **small** incremental amendments for three to five weeks. When your student is consistently fulfilling the contract, hold another meeting with the child. Acknowledge the improvement in the student's behavior. Ask the student whether the behavior has become routine or whether the contract is still needed. If you and the student determine that the contract is no longer needed, be sure to provide positive feedback when he or she continues to fulfill the goals on which the contract was previously based. If you terminate the contract too quickly or do not continue to verbally recognize your student, the child may slip back into the behaviors that initiated the contract in the first place. Before things deteriorate to their previous level, implement a new contract or reinstate the old one!

Engaging Other Caregivers in Cooperation Contracts. The same guidelines can be used for behavioral issues that are best handled by engaging more than one adult caregiver. The second adult may be a teacher's aide in your classroom or the child's parent(s). For example, problems related to homework may be more effectively managed if the child's parent is also a contracting partner. Issues around getting assignments to home and returned to school benefit from both settings working together, as the scenario in box 5.2 shows.

A contract with more than one caregiver can be a communication tool for the adults so that their respective roles and responsibilities can be clarified and coordinated. When parents are included in the contract, engage them in the negotiations. Reinforcements should be planned at school and home. You can download an empty child-parent-teacher contract from the website.

COOPERATION CONTRACTS FOR STUDENTS WITH ATTENTIONAL DIFFICULTIES

Students whose temperaments are low task persistence have attentional difficulties that complicate the academic demands of school. They have difficulty organizing and completing assignments, which is frustrating for them as well as their teachers. Cooperation Contracts can scaffold a student whose temperament is low in task persistence. For example, by beginning with a goal that has a realistic amount of concentration time attached to it, teachers can enhance their student's attention-related self-regulation. A timer can be set so that the student has a specific number of minutes for focusing on a task. Because such episodes will be taxing for the student, "take a break" should follow. Teachers need to provide students with low task persistence with positive feedback for their success or for their effort even when the goal has not been met.

COOPERATION CONTRACTS FOR CONFLICTUAL STUDENT-TEACHER RELATIONSHIPS

Cooperation Contracts are a particularly powerful tool to remediate conflict between a student and a teacher. A number of factors can contribute to a conflictual student-teacher relationship. Some children, regardless of their temperament, exhibit

BOX 5.2. A COOPERATION CONTRACT SCENARIO

Ms. Davis: Ms. Williams, I'm glad to see you again. I wanted to talk to you about Gregory's school work. He seems to be having trouble settling down at school.

Ms. Williams: What seems to be the problem?

Ms. Davis: He doesn't finish his work. He starts all right, but after a couple of minutes, he's doing anything else but his assigned work. How is he at home when he has homework?

Ms. Williams: Homework? He hasn't had homework. I always ask him, but he says he doesn't have any.

Ms. Davis: I'm glad we're meeting so I can tell you that the children have homework on Mondays, Tuesdays, Wednesdays, and Thursdays.

Ms. Williams: But Gregory says he always finishes his work at school.

Ms. Davis: Let me show you my grade book. See, here's Gregory's name. I've been keeping track of the children's homework over the last two weeks. Of the eight homework days, Gregory has handed in his homework only once.

Ms. Williams: He's kind of young to have homework, isn't he?

Ms. Davis: The children get about ten to fifteen minutes of homework. It is good for children his age to have some homework so that they develop good study habits.

Ms. Williams: It sounds to me as though Gregory's low persistence is interfering with his school work and with finishing things at home.

Ms. Davis: I have had success in circumstances like this with setting up a Cooperation Contract. It particularly works when the child's parent and I meet together with the child to set up the contract.

Ms. Williams: That's a great idea. Let's schedule a time, but before we meet with Gregory to make the contract, let's talk about how this works.

disruptive behavior such as being disrespectful to adults or physically aggressive with peers. Sometimes a teacher's attempts to change a student's disruptive behavior are ineffective. Instead the student remains noncompliant.

Teachers can also contribute to the conflict. A teacher might have unrealistic expectations given the child's temperament, developmental level, and/or aptitude. Of course, all teachers have days when they are overtired and stressed. Conflict can also be initiated by a teacher who responds counterproductively to a child who is acting benignly or who is being noncompliant. The student's temperament is likely to influence how he or she reacts to a teacher's irritated response. A child who is high in negative reactivity is likely to retort with an equally harsh remark that fuels the interchange and adds further momentum to the conflict. Moreover, some students have temperaments that are so high in negative reactivity that they frustrate most teachers.

Repeated incidents of conflict between a teacher and student have the propensity to accumulate until they escalate into deleterious interactions, a series of transactions that adversely affect the student-teacher relationship, the child's development, and teacher satisfaction. Over time, interactions like the ones just described are likely to result in a grim deadlock that is best described as *getting stuck*. Minor annoyances between the teacher and student will occur repeatedly until they escalate into high levels of conflict and misunderstanding. The transactions become more entrenched over time so that they can be initiated at the slightest provocation by the student or the teacher. The struggle eventually becomes so emotionally charged and embedded with negative expectations that it is easily evoked and often repeated. Student-teacher dyads engaged in this degree of struggle tend to continue to respond to each other in habitual, nonreflective ways that perpetuate the conflict (Mezirow, 1990).

"Getting stuck" has serious repercussions for the classroom. The teacher feels powerless when attempting to gain compliance from the student. The impact on the child is equally dramatic. Although it may not be obvious to the student, a child who is frequently successful in winning a power struggle with his or her teachers experiences a significant loss. Children expect the adults in their life to be more powerful than they are so that they can feel protected. If not, they lose confidence in the ability of their adult caregivers to help them behave in a manner that the child knows is socially acceptable.

A Cooperation Contract can "unstick" conflictual interactions between a teacher and student. Prior to implementing the contract, however, the teacher needs to carefully reflect on his or her part in maintaining the conflictual interactions (Teglasi, Simcox, & Kim, 2007). The teacher will also need to understand that the Cooperation Contracts will require a

---

Sidebar 5.1. Contracts Are Not Intended for a Personality Overhaul

Cooperation Contracts are designed to prompt small, incremental changes in a student's behavior. They are not intended for a personality overhaul. One of the impetuses for starting the *INSIGHTS for Teachers* program (McClowry et al., 2010) came from observing that some teachers were expecting radical changes in their students by implementing what they thought were contracts. The following example provides a verbatim listing of a behavior chart one teacher used with a student with a high maintenance temperament:

- Good work
- Good behavior
- Poor behaviors
- Out of seat
- Disrespectful to teacher
- Disruptive during lesson
- Throwing stuff around
- Fooling around
- Poor listening
- Excessive talking
- Incomplete work
- No homework

Needless to say, the student for whom the behavior chart was created was unsuccessful in meeting the teacher's goals!

concerted effort and patience. Successful contracts can resolve student noncompliance, reestablish the teacher's authoritative role in the classroom, and replace negative interchanges between the student and teacher with ones that are more positive. Both the student and the teacher benefit greatly!

SUMMARY

Self-regulation is defined in this chapter as the adaptive processes that individuals use to respond appropriately to the expectations and demands of their environment. Students who are high in self-regulation modulate their emotions, attention, and motor activities. As a result, they are often academically and socially successful.

Self-regulation develops over time. Infants initially rely on their parents for external regulation. As children get older, they apply effortful control to override their temperament tendencies in order to self-regulate. Students whose temperaments are high in task persistence and low in negative reactivity need to exert less effortful control to self-regulate than other children.

Classroom life presents students with temperamentally challenging situations that can enhance a student's self-regulation—especially when coupled with a teacher's support. Assessing the degree of challenge helps a teacher to decide whether to remove the child from the situation because it will be too distressful, or to scaffold the student with supportive stretching so that the student's self-regulation will be enhanced.

Teacher talk can provide students with cues for using effortful control to self-regulate. A more formalized teacher strategy to enhance student self-regulation is a Cooperation Contract, which is applicable for resolving student behavior problems, coordinating support among adult caregivers, supporting a student with attentional difficulties, and repairing a conflictual student-teacher relationship.

Implementing a Cooperation Contract begins with the selection of one feasible, positively stated goal. Then the student and teacher negotiate daily and weekly student responsibilities and daily and weekly reinforcements. The contract is formally signed by the student and teacher and kept in an agreed-upon location. While the contract is ongoing, the teacher should give no warnings. The student should be acknowledged when the daily and weekly responsibilities are fulfilled. No reprimands are given when the goal is not met. Instead a neutral statement encourages the student to try again the next time.

Students whose temperaments are low in task persistence benefit from Cooperation Contracts that encourage them to stretch their attention for short periods of time followed by a break. Cooperation Contracts also are a powerful tool for student-teacher relationships that have become conflictual. When successful, the contract can resolve the behavior problems of a frequently noncompliant student, reestablish the teacher's role in the classroom, and repair the student-teacher relationship.

In the next chapter, Cooperation Contracts will be briefly revisited as one of many teacher strategies that foster social competencies. Different developmentally appropriate approaches will be presented to support social competency skills related to listening, empathy, giving recognition, assertiveness, cooperation, problem-solving, dealing with anger, and conflict resolution.

CLASS DISCUSSION

- Role-play the development of a contract with one of your classmates.
- Discuss developmentally appropriate ways to tally positive contract-related behaviors.
- Examine the contract listed in sidebar 5.1 that was constructed by a teacher after repeated attempts to get compliance from a third grade child. Discuss why the contract is guaranteed to be unsuccessful.

OPTIONAL CASE STUDY ASSIGNMENT

If "Student C"'s teacher is agreeable, implement a Cooperation Contract with the student, teacher, and you. Revise the three-way contract on the website so it reflects who is involved.

RECOMMENDED READINGS

Baumeister, R. F., & Tierney, J. (2011). *Willpower: Rediscovering the greatest human strength.* New York, NY: The Penguin Press.

Denissen, J. J. A., van Aken, M. A. G., Penke, L., & Wood, D. (2013). Self-regulation underlies temperament and personality: An integrative developmental framework. *Child Development Perspectives, 7,* 255–260. doi:10.1111/cdep.12050

Vohs, K. D., & Baumeister, R. F. (2011). *Handbook of self-regulation: Research, theory, and applications* (2nd ed.). New York, NY: Guilford Press.

REFERENCES

Barros, R. M., Silver, E. J., & Stein, R. E. K. (2009). School recess and group classroom behavior. *Pediatrics, 123,* 431–436. doi:10.1542/peds.2007-2825

Baumeister, R. F., & Tierney, J. (2011). *Willpower: Rediscovering the greatest human strength.* New York, NY: The Penguin Press.

Denissen, J. J. A., van Aken, M. A. G., Penke, L., & Wood, D. (2013). Self-regulation underlies temperament and personality: An integrative developmental framework. *Child Development Perspectives, 7,* 255–260. doi:10.1111/cdep.12050

Eisenberg, N., Hofer, C., & Vaughan, J. (2007). Effortful control and its socioemotional consequences. In J. J. Gross (Ed.), *Handbook of emotion regulation* (pp. 287–306). New York, NY: Guilford Press.

Eisenberg, N., Smith, C. L., & Spinrad, T. L. (2011). Effortful control: Relations with emotion regulation, adjustment, and socialization in childhood. In R. F. Baumeister & K. D. Vohs (Eds.), *Handbook of self-regulation: Research, theory, and applications* (pp. 259–282). New York, NY: Guilford.

Frey, K. S., Nolen, S. B., Van Schoiack-Edstrom, L., & Hirschstein, M. K. (2005). Effects of a school-based social–emotional competence program: Linking children's goals, attributions, and behavior. *Applied Developmental Psychology, 26,* 171–200. doi:10.1016/j.appdev.2004.12.002

McClowry, S. G. (2003). *Your child's unique temperament: Insights and strategies for responsive parenting.* Champaign, IL: Research Press.

McClowry, S. G., Snow, D. L., Tamis-LeMonda, C. S., & Rodriguez, E. T. (2010). Testing the efficacy of *INSIGHTS* on student disruptive behavior, classroom management, and student competence in inner city primary grades. *School Mental Health, 2,* 23–35. doi:10.1007/s12310-009-9023-8

Mezirow, J. (1990). *Fostering critical reflection in adulthood: A guide to transformative and emancipatory learning.* San Francisco, CA: Jossey-Bass.

Miller, A. L., Gouley, K. K., Seifer, R., Dickstein, S., & Shields, A. (2004). Emotions and behaviors in the Head Start classroom: Associations among observed dysregulation, social competence, and preschool adjustment. *Early Education and Development, 15,* 147–165. doi:1 0.1207%2Fs15566935eed1502_2

O'Connor, E. E., Cappella, E., McCormick, M. P., & McClowry, S. G. (2013). *An examination of the efficacy of INSIGHTS in enhancing the academic learning context.* Manuscript submitted for publication.

Paris, S. G., & Paris, A. H. (2001). Classroom applications of research on self-regulated learning. *Educational Psychologist, 36,* 89–101. doi:10.1207%2FS15326985EP3602_4

Pelligrini, A., Huberty, P., & Jones, I. (1995). The effects of recess timing on children's playground and classroom behaviors. *American Educational Research Journal, 32,* 845–864. doi:10.3102%2F00028312032004845

Rothbart, M. K. (2011). *Becoming who we are: Temperament and personality in development.* New York, NY: Guilford Press.

Smart, D., Vassallo, S., Sanson, A., Richardson, N., Dussuyer, I., & McKendry, B. (2003). *Patterns and precursors of adolescent antisocial behavior: Type, resiliency, and environmental influences.* Melbourne, Australia: Australian Institute of Family Studies.

Teglasi, H., Simcox, A. G., & Kim, N. (2007). Personality constructs and measures. *Psychology in the Schools, 44,* 215–228. doi:10.1002%2Fpits.20218

CHAPTER 6

FOSTERING SOCIAL COMPETENCIES

ONCE UPON a time, long, long ago, Piglet turned to Pooh Bear and said: "'We'll be Friends Forever, won't we, Pooh?' and Pooh answered, 'Even longer.'" (Milne, 1996). Winnie the Pooh and Piglet were the original BFFs (Best Friends Forever).

Life, for children as well as adults, is enriched by friends. Finding a new friend is discovering a kindred spirit. The writer C. S. Lewis (1960) once said, "Friendship is born at that moment when one person says to another: 'What! You too? I thought I was the only one.'"

True friendships are alike in many ways (Ladd, 2005). Friends seek out each other's company. They have strong positive feelings toward each other and are sad when separated. Friends adjust their behavior to please the other. They help, comfort, and reassure each other.

Making friends in elementary school is an important developmental task that supports emotional maturation. Friends are chosen relationships that provide security outside the family (Rubin, Coplan, Chen, Bowker, & McDonald, 2011). Children explore the consequences of their behavior with their friends. In reciprocal ways, friendships teach children about intimacy and affection.

The friendships that children form—or do not develop—in elementary school have lasting imprints on their lives. Social competency skills are needed to initiate and maintain friendships and other positive peer relationships, such as those that occur among classmates or team members. This chapter focuses on the social competencies of elementary school students and the strategies that teachers can use to foster them. As will become evident in this chapter, students' social competencies are enhanced by teachers who are themselves socially competent.

IN THIS CHAPTER:

- Social competency is defined.
- The role of social competencies in enhancing relationships and academic achievement is discussed.
- A number of social competencies are presented with suggestions on how they can be demonstrated.
- Teacher strategies that foster the social competencies of their students are discussed.

DEFINING SOCIAL COMPETENCIES

A generic definition of competency is simply: "doing something well." Individuals who are competent have the knowledge and skills to perform well in their roles and to fulfill their responsibilities. Children are regarded as competent students when their academic performance is at least adequate. A comparable competency among adults is effective job performance.

One major category of competencies that supports a variety of functional roles is social. People who are socially competent integrate their emotions, cognitive skills, and behavior. As a result they can successfully adapt to life's challenges. Social competency skills include listening, empathy, cooperation and competition, problem-solving, conflict resolution, and assertiveness.

Denham and Brown (2010) enumerate the interactive components of social competencies expected of children in middle childhood:

- Self-awareness—identifying one's own feelings, interests, values, strengths, and limits
- Self-regulation—monitoring one's emotional state and intentional modulating of temperamental reactions (Rothbart, 2011)
- Social awareness of others—understanding and appreciating others' perspectives and empathizing with them
- Responsible decision making, including the ability to problem-solve and negotiate with peers and adults
- Evaluating the ethical repercussions of behavior and its impact on the well-being of others is a social competency that develops as children mature

THE COMPLEX WORLD OF CHILDREN'S RELATIONSHIPS

Elementary school provides many opportunities for children to expand their social competencies through interactions with their peers. Socially competent children learn subtle ways to interpret interpersonal cues (Cillessen & Bellmore, 2011). They understand how, when, and with whom they should share their emotions and ideas. When attempting to join an existing group of children, they cooperate by contributing to the activities of the group. As a result, they are well liked and accepted by their peers.

Not all children, however, are well liked. For instance, some children are "popular" but not necessarily well liked (Cillessen & Bellmore, 2011). Popular children have high peer status. They may be effective group leaders because they are assertive and can achieve their own goals or those of the group. However, the behavior of popular children can be perceived as socially aggressive and dominating. As a result, some peers may feel manipulated by a popular child.

Two other groups of children are not well liked and are labeled "rejected" (Cillessen & Bellmore, 2011). Peers reject other children who are aggressive and lacking in social skills. To complicate matters more, rejected children who are aggressive are inaccurate in their self-perceptions, so they may overestimate their acceptance by peers. As a result, they are unable to interpret their peers' verbal and nonverbal feedback, which if internalized, could improve their social skills. The other type of rejected children is "withdrawn." They lack the necessary social skills to engage with other children. Rejection by peers, whether due to aggressive or withdrawn behavior, has a detrimental effect on children's development.

ASSOCIATIONS BETWEEN SOCIAL COMPETENCIES AND OTHER OUTCOMES

Social competencies affect more than children's relationships. They interact reciprocally with academic outcomes (Nadeem, Maslak, Chacko, & Hoagwood, 2010). For example, rejected children often dislike school and make slower academic progress than their better-liked peers (Ladd, 2005). In contrast, social competencies promote classroom engagement, which in turn enhances academic achievement (Eisenberg, Valiente, & Eggum, 2010). Making a new friend in elementary school is associated with gains in school performance.

TEACHERS' ROLES IN SUPPORTING CHILD SOCIAL COMPETENCIES

The primary way that teachers foster the social skills of their students is by role-modeling their own socially competent behavior. Teachers who are self-aware recognize their own emotions and express them in ways that do not adversely affect their relationships with others (Jennings & Greenberg, 2009). They also encourage their students to identify and express their own emotions. If instead teachers give negative feedback when students express their emotions, children learn that their classroom is not an emotionally safe environment. As a result, some students will hide their emotions but feel anxious because they associate emotional expression with punishment.

Fostering the competency of students requires teachers to assess their own level of social competencies. Acquiring social competencies is a lifelong pursuit best regarded as "in progress." Remarkably, social competences are more similar for school-age children and adults than they are different. Everyone can benefit from fine-tuning one or more of the following social competencies regardless of one's age or role in life. After the competencies are presented, strategies are offered for adapting the content for your students.

Listening. Active listening demonstrates that you understand what the speaker said; it's more than just being quiet while someone is speaking. Listening is not achieved until the listener can reflect or summarize what the speaker said to the speaker's satisfaction. Here are a few hints on being a good listener:

- Pay attention to what the other person is telling you.
- Encourage the other person to tell you what he or she is thinking.
- Let your body language say that you are paying attention. Use good eye contact.
- Observe the other person's body language for other cues.
- Show the other person that you understand. For example, say something like:
  - *"That must have been difficult for you."*
  - *"I understand why you are frustrated."*
  - *"That is really exciting news!"*
- Ask questions when you do not understand what the other person is saying. For example, say something like:
  - *"I'm not sure I understand what you are saying. Can you give me more details?"*
  - *"Tell me more."*
- Provide validation by repeating what the other person said in your own words.

Empathy. Another social competency skill related to attentive listening is empathy. Empathy is an emotional response that matches another person's feelings or reaction to a distressful situation (Eisenberg et al., 2010). An empathic individual will feel sympathy and will express concern or sorrow for the other person. Altruistic behavior may follow. Some individuals experience emotional overarousal and personal distress in reaction to another's distress. Such an egotistical reaction is not socially competent and should not be confused with empathy. There are several ways to convey empathy:

- Restate what you heard the person say—not just the facts—but their perception or point of view.
- Identify the emotion that you believe the person is experiencing.
- Name the emotion you have identified.
- Respect the person's efforts to describe the emotion or situation.
- Use phrases that are empathetic:
  - "I hear you saying that . . ."
  - "So, as you see it . . ."
  - "I don't think that I've had the same experience, but it sounds like . . ."
  - "Are you telling me that you . . ."
  - "You sound concerned about . . ."
  - "Did you feel . . ."
- Offer emotional and/or tangible support.

Cooperation and competition. Another set of social competencies is cooperation and competition, which, at first glance, appear to be opposites. In actuality, cooperation and competition are often interwoven. Cooperation is a collaborative effort intended to benefit one's self as well as others (Schneider, Benenson, Fülöp, Berkics, & Sándor, 2011). The emphasis in competition, on the other hand, is on winning by outperforming others. A meta-analysis confirms that student cooperation, compared to competition, is associated with higher achievement and positive peer relationships (Roseth, Garfield, & Ben-Zvi, 2008).

In cross-cultural studies, Anglo-American children are the most competitive (Schneider et al., 2011). Moreover, boys are more competitive than girls, who, even in contemporary times, defer to boys' dominance.

Understanding how cooperation and competition can intertwine positively can help you foster your students' social and academic outcomes. Competition can be exciting and will enhance your students' intrinsic motivation if it encourages them to improve their individual skill levels (Schneider et al., 2011). Competing is particularly beneficial when there are clear rules and students have an equal opportunity to win and to gauge their own performance. Students who focus on self-improvement and mastery benefit more than those whose goal is to outperform others. Moreover, students who like each other and collaborate are more emotionally invested in the competitive event and satisfied even if their goals are not successful (Roseth et al., 2008). The following guidelines support cooperation intertwined with competition:

- Value your relationships with others.
- Be respectful of each other.
- Be clear about each person's roles and responsibilities.
- Have clear goals and rules when competing.
- Be flexible.
- Take turns.
- Acknowledge the skills and contributions of your team members.

Problem-solving, conflict resolution, and mediation. Even in classrooms where students value cooperation and use competition optimally, situations will arise that require a constructive process to resolve. Problem-solving, conflict management, and mediation are a hierarchy of related competency strategies that build upon each other. Increasing levels of emotions underscore each step of the hierarchy.

Two types of emotions exist (Izard, Stark, Trentacosta, & Schultz, 2008). Basic emotions, including anger, sadness, fear, and joy, occur automatically and unconsciously in infants and young children when a "life happens" event occurs. An emotional reaction and its depth emanate from the young child's temperament.

As children get older, they develop more complex emotional schemas based on their cognitive appraisals and the socialization experiences significant adults have provided. These emotional schemas modify or modulate the basic emotions and motivate a child toward a particular action. Children who are socially competent have emotional schemas based on accurate appraisals of their own emotions and those of

BOX 6.1. SOLVING DILEMMAS

Dilemmas are emotionally charged problems that may not have an ideal solution. Instead they require thinking and planning so that the best available option is implemented. When the primary grade children in *INSIGHTS* experience a conflict with their peers, they are encouraged to say: "Stop! We have a dilemma." If the other child agrees, he or she also responds with, "We have a dilemma." By agreeing that there is a dilemma, responsibility is shared for its resolution, cognitive problem-solving skills are activated, and emotions are tempered by exchanging frustration with logic and cooperation.

The children solve the dilemma with the assistance of puppets. There are several advantages for using puppets for solving dilemmas (Hall, Kaduson, & Schaefer, 2002). Puppets allow children to gain some emotional distance from the real-life situation, which makes the problem feel more manageable. The children use the puppets to

---

RED LIGHT
Stop: Recognize the dilemma.

What is the dilemma?

_____

YELLOW LIGHT
Caution: Think and plan.

Together come up with some ideas on how to handle the dilemma. Then discuss with each other whether each idea is good, medium, or bad.

_____	Good	Medium	Bad
_____	Good	Medium	Bad
_____	Good	Medium	Bad
_____	Good	Medium	Bad

GREEN LIGHT
Go: Try it out.

What happened? Did your plan solve the dilemma?

_____

_____

Table 6.1 Solving Dilemmas Worksheet

project their feelings, thoughts, and emotions. Another advantage is that the teacher can have insight into what the child is thinking and feeling as expressed by the puppets.

After acknowledging that that there is a dilemma, and guided by the Dilemma-Solving Worksheet shown in table 6.1 and the stoplight shown below, the puppets and the children "think and plan" by suggesting alternative actions to resolve their dilemma. Then they deliberate on each of the alternatives, deciding which is good, medium, or bad. The children continue to discuss their options until they agree on one and "try it out." During the next dilemma-solving classroom session, the children, or their representative puppets, are encouraged to report on how the solution worked. A videotaped vignette that demonstrates the dilemma-solving process is available on the website at www.insightsintervention.com.

Teachers in *INSIGHTS* hang a dilemma board in their classrooms. The visual reminder is readily available for the children to refer to when dilemmas are discussed during the weekly *INSIGHTS* classroom sessions. Some of the teachers also designate a space in their classrooms where the puppets are available for use when dilemmas occur.

INSIGHTS teachers report that after a few weeks of practice, the children use the dilemma-solving process independently. They have been observed interrupting older students on the playground who were clearly engaged in a dilemma with an assertive, "Stop! You have a dilemma," followed by instructions on how to resolve it. One group of children taught the dilemma-solving process to their principal when they found her in the hall dealing with an emotionally charged event.

Stop

Think
and plan

Try
it out

others. Other children, who are not socially competent, continue to operate from their basic emotions or from distorted emotional schemas.

"Life happens" events definitely arouse emotional schemas and sometimes evoke basic emotions. Implementing problem-solving and conflict management strategies modulates the emotional reaction by engaging in a cognitive activity. Problem-solving is a process that requires first thinking, then action (Izard et al., 2008). Thinking generates time to consider one or more options. A thoughtfully selected action is likely to be more socially competent than the one that emanated straight from an emotional reaction.

Children benefit from practicing a problem-solving strategy until it becomes a habit. Elias and Schwab (2006) maintain that once problem-solving becomes a consistent part of a child's cognitive tools, it is available for use throughout their lives whenever they encounter ethical, moral, or health dilemmas. Even young children can be taught to problem-solve as box 6.1 illustrates.

When problems are identified early and steps are taken to avoid their escalation, conflict may be avoided. Unfortunately that's not always the case. Conflict, which is often emotionally charged, is inevitable, especially among older children. Socially competent children gain from dealing with conflict as opposed to avoiding it. Conflict resolution occurs when everyone is satisfied with the outcome, the relationships among the involved parties are strengthened, and conflict resolution skills are enhanced (Johnson & Johnson, 2006). Older children benefit from having a more developmentally appropriate type of conflict resolution, as shown in table 6.2.

Sometimes, even if everyone involved tries to resolve a conflict, a mutually satisfying resolution may not occur. Mediation is recommended in such instances. An

Table 6.2. Guidelines for Conflict Resolution

1. Identify the conflict for yourself.
2. Try to understand why you are experiencing strong feelings in reaction to the conflict. What does it mean to you?
3. Apply all your social competency skills to resolve the conflict with your partner(s):   • Listening   • Empathy   • Assertiveness   • Cooperation
4. Acknowledge that the two of you have a conflict.
5. Discuss whether you agree about any issues related to the conflict.
6. Identify the parts on which you do not agree.
7. Discuss ideas on how you might resolve the conflict.
8. Select a solution that everyone can live with, even if it isn't everyone's first choice.
9. Set a time to check back with each other to see whether the solution is working.

impartial individual acts as the mediator and facilitates the conflict resolution process (Johnson & Johnson, 2006).

Assertiveness. Assertiveness is the ability to communicate clearly about one's interests and needs. Socially competent individuals are appropriately assertive. They maintain good boundaries with their friends and other peers by balancing cooperation with assertiveness.

Anger can be a sign that assertiveness is warranted (Izard et al., 2008). Psychological well-being is compromised when assertiveness is not interjected when it should be. Instead unnecessary anxiety or resentment may result when assertiveness is lacking.

School is a great place to practice assertiveness. Peers are equals, so children need to assert themselves to get their needs and desires met. An assertive person talks calmly and firmly when explaining what he or she wants to happen. Here are some pointers for being assertive:

- Express your opinion, values, and/or feelings by using "I" statements such as "I want . . . ," "I feel . . . ," or "I need . . ."
- Make sure the listener understands what you are saying. If he or she does not understand, explain it again.
- Use body language that relays that you are serious. Face the person directly but at a respectful distance while maintaining good eye contact.
- Use your voice effectively. Do not speak too softly or too loudly.
- Understand that you are responsible for yourself, your decisions, and your life choices.
- Recognize that being assertive is not always appreciated by others.

TEACHER STRATEGIES FOR FOSTERING YOUR STUDENTS' COMPETENCIES

The school year will present you with many opportunities to foster the social competencies of your students. There are at least three categories of pedagogical approaches you can use: (1) as a topic for discussion during a class meeting; (2) integrated into academic subjects; and (3) when situations naturally arise. As with any content, make sure that your teacher strategies are developmentally appropriate for your students. Here are some suggestions for using each of the categories with an encouragement to mix and match them to optimize their effects.

As a Class Meeting Topic. Socially competent students contribute to the community of learners. Class meetings, like those presented in chapter 4, can be devoted to a particular social competency. For example, you might teach your students about the importance of listening. To reinforce the content, give your students a listening exercise. Then reinforce the content when situations naturally arise.

The social competencies presented in this chapter progressively build upon each other. If you are going to introduce them in class meetings, it's best to present them in the sequence that they were introduced in this book. After all, effective resolution of conflicts requires listening, empathy, and cooperation.

Integrated into Academic Subjects. An excellent way to teach social competencies is to integrate them into academic lessons (Elias & Schwab, 2006). Providing your students with ample time to debate ideas and consider options and their consequences promotes student problem-solving skills (Stefanou, Perencevich, DiCintio, & Turner, 2004). Likewise errors become opportunities to clarify thinking processes and to reconsider options.

Reading class lends itself well for a discussion about social competencies. Characters in children's literature encounter all kinds of situations that demonstrate how social skills can resolve a dilemma and what happens when they are not employed. Social studies can also provide lessons on decision making by illuminating complex historical or sociological issues (Stevahn, Johnson, Johnson, & Schultz, 2002).

When situations naturally arise. Daily classroom life will provide ample opportunities to foster your students' social competencies. You can give gentle reminders to students when they encounter a challenging event that taxes their social competencies. A statement like "Sounds like you two are having a dilemma. Would you like to try resolving it with the problem-solving strategy we learned? Afterward, you can tell me how you chose to handle your dilemma." relays your confidence that the students can resolve the situation themselves.

Another way is to encourage your students to work cooperatively in group academic assignments and during social activities. You might also consider using peer-assisted learning strategies in which students tutor each other (Ginsburg-Block, Rohrbeck, Fantuzzo, & Lavigne, 2006). Students engaged in peer-assisted learning gain academically as well as socially.

You can also coach your students on handling difficult situations that are related to their temperaments. Students who are high in withdrawal, like Coretta the Cautious, have well-established cognitive schemas that interfere with peer interactions. Due to their high sensitivity, they often misinterpret their peers' actions and perceive themselves to be rejected (Coplan & Bullock, 2012). In turn, their reticence to engage invites other children to ignore them, further strengthening their cognitive schema that says they are rejected. Intentionally pairing a child who is high in withdrawal with an empathic peer may be an effective way of fostering peer support and weakening the cognitive schema.

Children who are high in negative reactivity are prone to appraising "life happens" events negatively and easily evoke conflict (Coplan & Bullock, 2012). Peers who are skilled in conflict resolution (and very patient) can assist children high in negative reactivity in working through their dilemmas. Be sure, however, to oversee the process so that children who are high in negative reactivity do not overpower their peers.

Students who are low in negative reactivity often need to be more assertive. They frequently are more concerned with pleasing other people than getting their own needs met, as the scenario in box 6.2 demonstrates. Ms. Davis can respond to this situation counterproductively, adequately, or optimally.

BOX 6.2. HILARY HAS A DILEMMA

Ms. Davis's class is working on their art project. Ms. Davis notices that a number of the children are asking Hilary to help them with their project by requesting that she give them supplies. Hilary is graciously responding to their requests and as a result is not making much progress on her own project.

On one hand, she appreciates that Hilary is trying to be helpful to her friends. But Ms. Davis is also concerned that Hilary is not being assertive. Instead, she is engaged in the helper role at her own expense. If Ms. Davis scolds Hilary by remarking, "Hilary, what's the matter with you? Why aren't you making any progress on your art project? You are spending all your time helping the other kids," she uses a counterproductive response. By reacting harshly to the situation, Ms. Davis conveys criticism. Hilary is likely to be confused by her teacher's remarks because being helpful is an attribute that Hilary values about herself and about which she usually gets positive reinforcement. Even though Ms. Davis's motivation might be to encourage her student to be more assertive, Hilary is likely to feel that she is being reprimanded.

ICON 6.1

Teacher responses that are counterproductive make the situation worse; adequate responses resolve the situation quickly; and optimal responses enhance the competency of the student in addition to resolving the situation.

A different strategy would be for Ms. Davis to intervene by gently reminding the other children that Hilary needs time to work on her own project. Such a response is only adequate because although it resolves the immediate situation, it doesn't help Hilary become more assertive.

An optimal teacher response would be to first help Hilary find a comfortable place from which she can do her art project. A discussion regarding Hilary's lack of assertiveness could be handled later. Ms. Davis will need to find a quiet time and private space to discuss what happened so that Hilary doesn't feel she is being reprimanded (see box 6.3).

Ms. Davis's challenge in this scenario was to let Hilary know that she was not criticizing her for being helpful, but was concerned that her lack of assertiveness compromised her opportunity to finish her own work. In sharp contrast to the counterproductive exchange that was previously described, Ms. Davis discussed the issue in a sensitive way and used an empathic rather than a critical tone of voice.

BOX 6.3. LEARNING HOW TO BE ASSERTIVE

Ms. Davis: Hilary, how do you think your arts project is coming along?
Hilary: It's okay.
Ms. Davis: I'm glad that you are working on it, but I'm concerned that you didn't get a chance to finish your project because you were helping all the other kids.
Hilary: Well that's okay, because the other kids needed colored papers and paste to finish their pictures.
Ms. Davis: Still, it wasn't fair to you that most of your time was spent helping them. You deserved the opportunity to work on your own project as much as they did. What do you think you could do the next time we have art class so that you can finish your own project?

SUMMARY

In this chapter, social competency is defined as the integration of emotions, cognitive skills, and behavior that contribute to successful adaptations to life's challenges. Social competencies support the initiation and maintenance of friendships and other peer relationships. Rather than being separate from academic outcomes, social competencies reciprocally interact with student achievement. Having good friends supports children in their academic pursuits and in growing their social competencies. Although peers have a major role in the development of social competencies, teachers who are socially competent serve as excellent role models.

Social competencies are similar for adults and students. Everyone can be challenged to enhance at least one of their social competency skills. Active listeners accurately summarize what a speaker has said. Empathic individuals feel sympathy or concern for another person, often offering support or tangible help. Cooperation and competition, when interwoven, support relationships.

Problem-solving, conflict resolution, and mediation require both emotional awareness and using logic. Engaging in a problem-solving process reduces emotional reactions to "life happens" situations and can facilitate the selection of positive choices when encountering dilemmas. Problem-solving also can prevent minor problems from advancing into conflict situations coupled with strong emotionally charged reactions. A successful conflict resolution in which all parties are satisfied with the outcome can strengthen relationships and should not be avoided. If conflict resolution is not successful, mediation by an impartial person may be needed. Assertiveness, the ability to clearly communicate one's interests and needs, is another social competency that supports psychological well-being.

Teachers can foster the social competencies of their students with multiple pedagogical strategies. They can discuss and provide practice opportunities for their students to demonstrate social competency skills during class meetings. Academic subjects can also be integrated with social competency lessons. Situations will naturally arise in classroom life that will provide other opportunities to foster the social competencies of students. Using a temperament lens, teachers can recognize when students need support from them or their peers in order to expand their social competency repertoire.

CLASS DISCUSSION

- Tell your student-colleagues about your best friend in elementary school. If you are not in contact with him or her, consider using a social media site to reconnect.
- Go on the following website and explore other quotes about friendship: http://www.cloverquotes.com/about/friendship. Find a quote that is particularly meaningful to you. Discuss with your student-colleagues why you selected that quote.
- Role-play resolving other dilemmas listed on http://www.insightsintervention.com.

COURSE ASSIGNMENTS

- Select a social competency skill that you think you could improve. Set a goal for yourself for the next week. If you feel comfortable doing so, report back on your own progress in enhancing a social competency skill.
- Find a developmentally appropriate example in literature or in a social studies lesson that demonstrates how an outcome was influenced by a social competency.

OPTIONAL CASE STUDY ASSIGNMENT

Observe "Student E" and "Student C" this week for episodes of social competence.

1. Write down a time when he or she acted in a socially competent way.
2. Did you give the student recognition?
3. How did the student react if you acknowledged his or her competency?

RECOMMENDED READINGS

Coplan, R. J., & Bullock, A. (2012). Temperament and peer relationships. In R. Shiner & M. Zentner (Eds.), *Handbook of childhood temperament* (pp. 442–461). New York, NY: Guilford Press.

Denham, S. A., & Brown, C. (2010). "Plays nice with others": Social-emotional learning and academic success. *Early Education and Development, 21*(5), 652–680. doi:10.1080/10409 289.2010.497450

Jennings, P., & Greenberg, M. T. (2009). The prosocial classroom: Teacher social and emotional competence in relation to student and classroom outcomes. *Review of Educational Research, 79*, 491–525. doi:10.3102/0034654308325693

Milne, A. A. (1996). *The Complete Winnie-the-Pooh and the House at Pooh Corner.* New York, NY: Dutton Children's.

REFERENCES

Cillessen, A. H. K., & Bellmore, A. (2011). Social skills and social competence in interactions with peers. In P. K. Smith & C. H. Hart (Eds.), *The Wiley-Blackwell handbook of childhood social development* (2nd ed., pp. 393–412). Malden, MA: Wiley.

Coplan, R. J., & Bullock, A. (2012). Temperament and peer relationships. In R. Shiner & M. Zentner (Eds.), *Handbook of childhood temperament* (pp. 442–461). New York, NY: Guilford Press.

Denham, S. A., & Brown, C. (2010). "Plays nice with others": Social-emotional learning and academic success. *Early Education and Development, 21*(5), 652–680. doi:10.1080/10409289 .2010.497450

Eisenberg, N., Valiente, C., & Eggum, N. D. (2010). Self-regulation and school readiness. *Early Education & Development, 21*(5), 681–698. doi:10.1080/10409289.2010.497451

Elias, M. J., & Schwab, Y. (2006). From compliance to responsibility: Social and emotional learning and classroom management. In C. M. Evertson & C. S. Weinstein (Eds.), *Handbook of classroom management: Research, practice, and contemporary issues* (pp. 309–341). Mahwah, NJ: Lawrence Erlbaum Associates Publishers.

Ginsburg-Block, M., Rohrbeck, C., Fantuzzo, J., & Lavigne, N. C. (2006). Peer-assisted learning strategies. In G. Bear & K. M. Minke (Eds.), *Children's needs III: Development, prevention, and intervention* (pp. 631–645). Washington, DC: National Association of School Psychologists.

Hall, T. M., Kaduson, H. G., & Schaefer, C. E. (2002). Fifteen effective play therapy techniques. *Professional Psychology: Research and Practice, 33*, 515–522. doi:10.1037/0735 -7028.33.6.515

Izard, C. E., Stark, K., Trentacosta, C., & Schultz, D. (2008). Beyond emotion regulation: Emotion utilization and adaptive functioning. *Child Development Perspectives, 2*(3), 156–163. doi:10.1111/j.1750-8606.2008.00058.x

Jennings, P., & Greenberg, M. T. (2009). The prosocial classroom: Teacher social and emotional competence in relation to student and classroom outcomes. *Review of Educational Research, 79*, 491–525. doi:10.3102/0034654308325693

Johnson, D. W., & Johnson, R. T. (2006). Conflict resolution, peer mediation, and peacemaking. In C. M. Evertson & C. S. Weinstein (Eds.), *Handbook of classroom management* (pp. 803–832). Mahwah, NJ: Lawrence Erlbaum Associates Publishers.

Ladd, G. W. (2005). *Children's peer relations and social competence: A century of progress.* New Haven, CT: Yale University Press.

Lewis, C. S. (1960). *The Four Loves* (p. 78). New York, NY: Harcourt Brace.

Milne, A. A. (1996). *The complete Winnie-the-Pooh and the House at Pooh Corner.* New York, NY: Dutton Children's.

Nadeem, E., Maslak, K., Chacko, A., & Hoagwood, K. E. (2010). Aligning research and policy on social-emotional and academic competence for young children. *Early Education & Development, 21*(5), 765–779. doi:10.1080/10409289.2010.497452

Poduska, J., Gomez, M., Capo, Z., & Holmes, V. (2012). Developing a collaboration with the Houston Independent School District: Testing the generalizability of a partnership model. *Administration and Policy in Mental Health and Mental Health Services Research, 39*(4), 258–267. doi:10.1007/s10488-011-0383-7

Roseth, C. J., Garfield, J. B., & Ben-Zvi, D. (2008). Collaboration in learning and teaching statistics. *Journal of Statistics Education, 16*(1), 1–15.

Rothbart, M. K. (2011). *Becoming who we are*. New York, NY: The Guildford Press.

Rubin, K. H., Coplan, R., Chen, X., Bowker, J., & McDonald, K. L. (2011). Peer relationships in childhood. In M. H. Bornstein & M. E. Lamb (Eds.), *Developmental science: An advanced textbook* (6th ed., pp. 519–570). New York, NY: Psychology Press.

Schneider, B. H., Benenson, J., Fülöp, M., Berkics, M., & Sándor, M. (2011). Competition and cooperation. In C. Hart and P. K. Smith (Eds.), *Handbook of child social development*, (2nd ed., pp. 472–490). Malden, MA: Wiley.

Stefanou, C. R., Perencevich, K. C., DiCintio, M., & Turner, J. C. (2004). Supporting autonomy in the classroom: Ways teachers encourage student decision making and ownership. *Educational Psychologist*, *39*(2), 97–110. doi:10.1207/s15326985ep3902_2

Stevahn, L., Johnson, D. W., Johnson, R. T., & Schultz, R. (2002). Effects of conflict resolution training integrating into a high school social studies curriculum. *Journal of Social Psychology*, *142*(3), 305–331. doi:10.1080/00224540209603902

Tingstrom, D. H., Sterling-Turner, H. E., & Wilczynski, S. M. (2006). The good behavior game: 1969–2002. *Behavior Modification*, *30*, 225–253. doi:10.1177/0145445503261165

THE 3 Rs AND THE 2 Ss REAPPLIED TO TEACHERS

IN PART III of this book, the previously presented content is reexamined for its applicability to teachers. The 3 Rs of Recognize, Reframe, and Respond and the 2 Ss of Scaffold and Stretch are revisited. This time, the related strategies are intended to assist teachers in their role as educators and in their own social-emotional development. After all, teachers are people, too!

CHAPTER 7

TEACHERS ARE PEOPLE, TOO

ALMOST all teachers are deeply concerned about their students and are committed to advancing their academic and socioemotional development. Sometimes the day-to-day demands of being a teacher can, however, feel burdensome. This chapter is an honest examination of the struggles that teachers invariably encounter trying to meet the seemingly unending requests and idiosyncratic needs of students and their parents in addition to their other work requirements. Many teachers' reactions to the juggling of responsibilities can be encapsulated in two statements: "I need a break" and "This is not how I expected teaching to be."

The earlier chapters of this book presented teacher strategies intended to enhance the development of your students and your relationships with their families and your colleagues. In this chapter, the same mnemonics of the 3 Rs (Recognize, Reframe, and Respond) and the 2 Ss (Scaffold and Stretch) are reexamined for their applicability to teachers. Used consistently, these strategies are expected to make your teaching career more fulfilling and enjoyable—and benefit your students as well.

IN THIS CHAPTER:

- **Recognize** your own temperament and related emotions.
- **Reframe** your perspectives so that career challenges become opportunities.
- **Respond** effectively to students with challenging temperaments and to stressful situations.
- **Scaffold** yourself when ongoing stressors occur.
- **Stretch** your knowledge base and your own social competencies.

> ### BOX 7.1. THE HOLIDAYS ARE COMING!
> ### THE HOLIDAYS ARE COMING!
>
> Imagine this scenario. It's the last day of school before a big holiday vacation. Your students could *not* be more excited! The noise level in your classroom is reaching a crescendo. You realize the students need to expend some of their energy, but there's an unrelenting rainstorm. Everyone will need to stay in the building today.
>
> Your personal life is adding to the day's stressors. You have not finished your holiday shopping, and for reasons that you can no longer fathom, you volunteered to host your family's holiday party. Surely these factors are contributing to your headache. So, you take a deep breath and assure yourself that the school day will end soon. Then you look at the clock. The time is 10:15 a.m. Oh, dear!

THE FIRST OF THE 3 Rs: RECOGNIZE

Teachers are people, too. They have their own array of needs, interests, and—their own temperaments. In the same way that recognizing the temperament of your students is a precursor for selecting teacher strategies to support their socioemotional and academic development, recognizing your own temperament and its related emotions is an important step in enhancing your own well-being.

Teaching is emotional. Surveys consistently identify a number of factors that contribute to the myriad of feelings teachers have about their jobs (Carson, Baumgartner, Matthews, & Tsouloupas, 2010). They include disruptive classroom behavior, the level of support they receive from their principals, competing job demands, interpersonal relations with colleagues, availability of resources, high-stakes student testing, and relationships with their students' parents.

When examined and understood, emotions provide a great deal of information about oneself. Emotions arise in response to someone or to an event and can range from low intensity to high (Van Kleef, Homan, & Cheshin, 2012). The intensity of the response is related to the relevance of the situation to an individual and to one's temperament. Teachers whose temperaments are high in negative reactivity react more strongly and negatively than those who are low on that trait (Montgomery & Rupp, 2005). For example disruptive students are likely to evoke negative emotions in most teachers (Jennings & Greenberg, 2009). However, while some teachers feel enraged, others are annoyed, and still others just a little displeased. Teachers also have a range of positive emotions. For example, if a student with reading problems finally shows substantial progress, a teacher might feel exuberant, or perhaps, delighted, or maybe just pleased.

Typically, emotions are short-lived. In contrast, moods last longer and are not related to a specific person or event, but are more diffuse (Van Kleef et al., 2012). Being in a particular mood state, however, is likely to trigger a reaction or attitude. For example, a teacher who is in a good mood on a particular day is likely to enjoy her students more than if her mood is gloomy.

Accepting, not judging, your emotional reactions is the key to a deeper recognition of their underlying meanings. If you recognize that your emotional reactions make sense in light of how you perceive the situation, your insight into your feelings will grow. Taking a closer look at your emotions and their underlying meaning will also lead to actions that are more deliberate and genuine.

All teachers juggle multiple responsibilities at their schools. Yet, teachers respond to their jobs in different ways. Some teachers are more distressed by the same circumstances than others. Stress occurs when the demands of a situation exceed one's ability to cope (Lazarus & Folkman, 1984). In other words, one's perception of the event largely determines the level of stress experienced. This conclusion was supported in an elegant study of 451 teachers from thirteen urban and suburban elementary schools (McCarthy, Lambert, O'Donnell, & Melendres, 2009). Although the schools differed substantially in the socioeconomic status of the students they served, available resources, and administrative support, there was little variation in the amount of stress the teachers reported between the schools. Instead, the individual teachers' perceptions were the primary contributors to their stress level—regardless of the school factors.

Because teachers are adults, their reactions to situations and people are more complicated and multifaceted than those of children. Motivation and self-esteem substantially contribute to a teacher's emotions and reactions. For example, while disruptive student behavior is stressful for most teachers (Sutton, Mudrey-Camino, & Knight, 2009), the reasons for their reactions vary. One teacher might feel discouraged by her classroom management skills. Another might be worried that the principal will judge him harshly and it will adversely affect his job. A third teacher might feel frustrated with the students. Many teachers will experience a number of feelings simultaneously.

THE SECOND OF THE 3 Rs: REFRAME YOUR PERCEPTIONS

Stressors can, however, be reframed as opportunities.

Rather than becoming discouraged or frustrated, some teachers regard their career challenges positively. Teachers who are high in self-efficacy (Bandura, 1997) are energized and determined to resolve the associated problems (Schwarzer & Hallum, 2008).

They set goals for themselves and are persistent in achieving them. They also recover more quickly when they experience adversity. Not surprisingly, student learning is greater in classrooms with teachers that are high in self-efficacy compared to those who perceive themselves as inadequate (Schwarzer & Hallum, 2008).

ICON 7.1

Reframing is changing one's perspective so that the reinterpretation incorporates an expanded and more nuanced interpretation.

THE LAST OF THE 3 RS: RESPOND

As already acknowledged, disruptive student behavior is a stressor for teachers (Kokkinos, Panayiotou, & Davazoglou, 2005). Students who are withdrawn or unengaged can also be taxing. So can students who are very energetic. The following sections list advanced strategies for effectively responding to students who have a variety of temperaments.

ICON 7.2

Self-efficacy is the perception that one is capable of handling a situation (Bandura, 1997).

Responding to Students Whose Temperaments Are Eager to Try. Children whose temperaments are eager to try (low in withdrawal) need constant monitoring to ensure their safety. These children are intrigued with the opportunity to engage in escapades. Monitoring eager-to-try students can be particularly stressful while on field trips or in other situations that take your students out of the contained environment of the classroom. Here are some advanced strategies for dealing with students who are eager to try:

- Appreciate how enthusiastically students who are eager enjoy life!
- Carefully balance the desire of eager-to-try students' excitement with your commitment to keep them safe.
- Plan strategies that are appropriate to your students' developmental age when embarking on field trips. For younger students, assign a parent to carefully monitor them. Discuss expectations for safe behavior with older students (and the consequences for not following such guidelines).
- Capitalize on the exuberance of children who are eager to try. Use it to energize other students when engaged in group assignments.

Responding to Students Whose Temperaments Are Slow to Warm. Children whose temperaments are slow to warm (high in the withdrawal dimension) often react to subtle cues or to situations that most individuals do not even notice. They also are *very* sensitive to people and their environments; their feelings are easily hurt even though they may not articulate their emotions. Here are some advanced strategies for dealing with students who are slow to warm:

- Appreciate that a child who is slow to warm can be counted upon to observe things in life that most people miss.
- Learn to read your student's subtle cues that signal when he or she is in need of reassurance or when a situation is too distressful and should not be pursued.
- Encourage your student to express his or her feelings and needs.

- Students who are slow to warm respond well when you scaffold and stretch. For example, ease your student into new situations by remaining positive, preparing the student for the event, and by linking it to comfortable elements such as mentioning how this activity is similar to a previous one.
- Acknowledge your students' progress.

Responding to Students Whose Temperaments Are High in Negative Reactivity. Students who are high in negative reactivity are challenging for most teachers, especially when teachers take their negative reactivity personally. Remember that a child who is high in negative reactivity cannot be changed into a sunny person; trying to do so will only frustrate you and your student. Here are some advanced strategies for dealing with a child who is high in negative reactivity:

- Briefly and calmly acknowledge the reason the child is distressed. Then quickly redirect the conversation toward something more positive.
- Remind yourself that you do not respond to every complaint. Giving too much attention to the child's negative reactivity convinces the child that negative reactivity is a powerful tool to control other people.
- As a teacher you have the right to expect respectful behavior from your students. Be clear about the types of verbal or nonverbal expressions that are acceptable in your classroom.
- Expect compliance even if it is accompanied by an expression of negative reactivity as long as it is expressed in a reasonable way.
- Focus on gaining the student's compliance while ignoring his or her attitude. In other words, concentrate on the issue, not on the child's expression of dissatisfaction.
- If you know that some disappointing news is likely to be very distressful to your student, forewarn the child that you have information to talk about that may be upsetting. Encourage the student to take some time before responding. If the child immediately reacts, ignore the first reaction and give the student another opportunity to provide a more socially appropriate response.
- Give yourself time before you respond to a child who is high in negative reactivity.
- Garnish emotional support from other adults to reduce your own frustration with dealing with a child who is high in negative reactivity.

Responding to Students Whose Temperaments Are Low in Task Persistence. Children who are low in task persistence have difficulty completing assignments. Here are some advanced strategies for dealing with such a child:

- Be sure to make eye contact with your student and wait until he or she is attentive before you give a directive.
- Prepare assignments appropriate to the child's academic level. If the assignment is too difficult, a child who is low in task persistence will be overwhelmed and will

not complete the activity. If, however, the assignment is too easy, the child will be become bored and will not stay engaged.

- Decide which assignments are important versus those are repetitious and inconsequential and do not require completion.
- Divide complicated assignments into smaller, more-manageable tasks. Help your student organize the assignment with a time line.
- Consider using a timer so your student knows how long he or she is required to work on each assignment. (Some children respond well to the challenge of finishing the task before the timer rings.)
- Acknowledge your student when he or she has completed a task. Then immediately move on to the next one to keep up the momentum or provide a brief break between tasks.
- If your student has a choice of assignments, assist him or her in selecting one that he or she finds interesting.
- Alternate learning activities that require concentration with ones that are less demanding.
- Children who are low in task persistence often cooperate with behavior contracts when they include manageable goals and tangible reinforcements.
- Keep in close contact with your student's parent(s) regarding school and home assignments. Better yet, engage the student's parents in a behavior contract.
- Encourage after-school or at-home activities that foster an increased amount of sustained concentration (like chess or other similar board games) rather than those that require quick reactions (like video games).
- Although children who are low in task persistence need you to provide consistency and structure, do not expect them to be grateful, especially if they are also high in negative reactivity.

Responding to Students Whose Temperaments Are High in Activity. Children who are high in motor activity seem to be in motion all of the time. Even when they are supposed to be sitting still, they manage to wiggle or bounce in their seat. Here are some advanced strategies for dealing with a child who is high in activity:

- Provide opportunities for physical or sports-related activities so that the child's high activity level has a suitable outlet. Otherwise, their need for activity may bubble over into inappropriate situations like during a reading lesson or other quiet classroom times.
- Consider offering other ways to complete assignments if sitting in a chair is very difficult for your student. Some highly active students work better if allowed to stand or sit on a large ball rather than at their desks. Such privileges, of course, require that the student be respectful of the other students' space. Consideration for the comfort of other students must be taken into account.

Responding to Students Whose Temperaments Are High Maintenance. Students with high maintenance temperaments are especially challenging and require a great deal of patience. A child who is high maintenance needs you to be his or her advocate. Unfortunately, this role may further increase your feelings of being burdened. Use a combination of the strategies that have already been suggested for children who are high in negative reactivity, low in task persistence, and high in activity. Here are some additional advanced strategies for dealing with students whose temperaments are high in negative reactivity.

- Understand that child behavior contracts will need to be used for an extended period of time, even after your student appears to have changed a particular behavior.
- Provide generous amounts of warmth, frequent reinforcements, and affirmation for positive behavior.

Responding to Dilemmas. In addition to responding to challenging students, teachers have to deal with ethical and professional dilemmas that are not easily resolved.

In the course of their workweek, teachers face many dilemmas that can compromise teaching practices if left unresolved (Helsing, 2007). An example of a teacher dilemma is deciding how much individual instruction to give a child who is struggling to learn compared to the rest of the students, who are making steady progress. Another common dilemma is allocating time for preparing students for state exams rather than expanding on a topic in which the students are fully engaged.

ICON 7.3

Dilemmas are emotionally charged problems that may not have an ideal resolution. Instead they require thinking and planning so that the best available option can be chosen.

The best way to respond to a dilemma is by applying a problem-solving strategy. Similar to the one presented in chapter 6 for children, the teacher version of problem-solving begins with clearly identifying the dilemma but then explores why the dilemma poses difficulties for you. When possible, don't rush into a decision. Then take time to consider alternatives. You may benefit from consulting with trusted colleagues before you respond so that you can discern the best possible resolution (Helsing, 2007).

Delayed responses are optimal in other situations as well. In chapter 4, time-out was presented as a strategy to improve student compliance because it provides an opportunity to cool down and then resume activities in a less-reactive way. If your temperament is high in negative reactivity, you probably noticed that taking time to cool down before you respond is beneficial. Even teachers who are low in negative reactivity may need an occasional time-out. Not only do time-outs provide a brief respite, but they also model to your students how you self-regulate your responses.

Two types of teacher time-out are listed below:

- *Time-out before responding:* a ten-second pause before you decide how you will respond to a specific student's behavior or to the classroom as a whole. To implement this strategy, say to the student or the classroom, "I need to think about this for a minute."
- *Major time-out:* recommended when a student's behavior or the classroom situation is serious enough to warrant careful thinking or when you are too angry to respond thoughtfully. To implement this strategy, say something like, "I will deal with this after lunch when I have had time to think."

ICON 7.4

Self-regulation is the adaptive processes that individuals use to respond appropriately to the expectations and demands of the environment.

THE FIRST OF THE 2 Ss: SCAFFOLD

When ongoing stressors occur, more than a time-out is necessary. Scaffolding yourself is recommended so that the associated distress does not escalate into a more serious problem.

Burnout can occur when teachers feel unrelenting stress for a long time. Symptoms of teacher burnout are emotional and physical exhaustion, withdrawing from students and colleagues, cynicism, irritability, and a reduced sense of professional accomplishment (Maslach & Jackson, 1981). Some teachers are more susceptible to burnout than others. Not surprisingly, teachers who are at risk for emotional exhaustion have temperaments that are high in negative reactivity (Carson et al., 2010). Another group of teachers who are at risk for burnout are those who set overly ambitious goals and have unrealistic expectations of themselves.

ICON 7.5

Scaffolding in respect to teachers is being able to maintain equilibrium during difficult circumstances.

Supportive environments provide scaffolding accompanied with the right amount and type of stimulation. Just like children, adults benefit when they experience goodness of fit.

Fortunately, the teaching field provides many options for teachers as they advance in their career. The ideal position provides goodness of fit for a teacher's particular temperament. For example, while some teachers prefer schools with a homogeneous student body, others desire more diversity among their students.

Goodness of fit for teachers is related to several other school factors (Bevans, Bradshaw, Miech, & Leaf, 2007). Consistent school discipline and a strong emphasis on academics are associated with teacher job satisfaction. Other positive school environment factors include warm and helpful relationships among teacher colleagues and principals who are open to the ideas of their teaching staff. New teachers in urban schools particularly benefit from a school environment that encourages collaboration (Chester & Beaudin, 1996). They also gain when their principals observe their teaching and offer their wisdom and suggestions for further development.

Other scaffolding strategies are more intrapsychic. Sometimes it helps just to realign one's expectations. Experienced teachers report that during trying times they frequently remind themselves: "They're just kids" (Sutton et al., 2009).

Another strategy is to review why you became a teacher. As discussed in chapter 4, your relationship with the students in your class can positively affect their emotional and academic outcomes.

ICON 7.6

Goodness of fit occurs when the demands, expectations, and opportunities of the environment match an individual's temperament (Chess & Thomas, 1984).

The influence you have on your students can have a major impact on their lives years after they have left your classroom. Effective elementary school teachers make a difference (Chetty, Friedman, & Rockoff, 2011). Their students are more likely to attend college, earn higher salaries, live in better neighborhoods, and are less likely to have children while still teenagers. Students with disruptive behavior and those who are from low-income homes especially benefit from a supportive teacher (Jennings & Greenberg, 2009).

ICON 7.7

You are important to your students!

You can also use a number of common-sense, pragmatic strategies to scaffold your health and mental health. Eat nutritious foods, exercise regularly, and get enough sleep at night. Keep your classroom organized so that you feel better prepared to handle the day's opportunities and challenges. Wisely use social and tangible support from your family, friends, and colleagues (Montgomery & Rupp, 2005). Remember that venting to a receptive friend or family member can rejuvenate you after a long day. Meeting with a mental health professional is yet another scaffolding strategy.

Dedication to students and the teaching profession is highly commendable but must be balanced with self-care. Ironically, another way to effectively deal with the multiple responsibilities that teachers have is to take a break from them. Teachers need time away to revive themselves. Otherwise, they are likely to be exhausted and impatient with their students and unsatisfied with their professional life as well as their personal life.

"Taking a break" is time dedicated just to you. To employ this strategy, intentionally plan opportunities to refresh and renew yourself. Schedule a break so that you have an uninterrupted period of time even if you can realistically only count on a half hour—or even fifteen minutes. Also, be sure to plan a longer break time during holidays and summer vacations. It is especially important to take a break when you recognize that you often feel hassled or tired. A break can leave you feeling more poised so that you can respond more thoughtfully and competently in your interactions with others.

If you are the type of person who takes great pride in fulfilling your responsibilities, you may be prone to neglecting yourself or may deny that you actually *need* a break. In our *INSIGHTS* program, teachers are given an assignment to give themselves a break. Ironically, although not unexpectedly, the teachers who were the most responsible in completing student-centered assignments have the most difficulty fulfilling this one. You also may have difficulty taking a break unless you are convinced that renewing yourself benefits you and your students. Experiment! Give yourself a break and see whether you experience a renewed energy and sense of satisfaction.

In reality, deadlines and their related stressors often come in bunches and leave little time for taking a break. For example, the end of the school year brings a flurry of competing demands like finishing paperwork and student records, calculating your students' final grades, preparing report cards, and packing up your classroom materials. During such intense times, higher levels of scaffolding are required. Place yourself in a self-imposed "protective custody." Here are some helpful suggestions for weathering such intense times:

- Realize that you will be easily annoyed by situations and people. Try not to take your assessments of others or yourself too seriously.
- Make no major decisions while in protective custody unless they are absolutely unavoidable. For example, don't quit your teaching job, end a long-term relationship, or join the circus!

A couple of weeks after the intense period has ended, take time to review the situation and your associated reactions. Ask yourself several questions: What did you learn about yourself? Did you use any scaffolding strategies that helped you? Were there other strategies you wished you had implemented? What do you plan to do differently the next time? Make a plan for stretching yourself so that you will be better prepared the next time.

THE SECOND OF THE 2 Ss: STRETCH

Adults who consider themselves fully grown are missing out on wonderful opportunities to **stretch** themselves. Learning, as one example, should be a never-ending quest, especially for teachers. There are a number of ways that teachers can continue learning new things. Taking college courses is one option. Other ways to continue learning include reading professional journals and exchanging ideas with other teachers. Also, take advantage of opportunities to learn something that is unrelated to your job. Be aware, however, that "unrelated" content may percolate, when you least expect it, into creative ideas for your classroom.

Another way to enhance your teaching is through professional development programs that will benefit you and enhance student achievement (Yoon, Duncan, Lee, Scarloss, & Shapley, 2007). The most effective types of professional development programs are evidence based, are at least fourteen hours long, and include follow-up activities.

Stretching pertains to more than the cognitive domain. Enhancing one's social competency skills should be a lifelong pursuit.

As discussed in the last chapter, social competency skills are best regarded as "in progress." Everyone can stretch at least one of their social competencies, which include listening, empathy, cooperation, competition, problem-solving, conflict management, and mediation.

ICON 7.8

Social competency is the integration of emotions, cognitive skills, and behavior that supports a successful adaptation to life's challenges.

Stretching your social competencies benefits you and your students. When compared to children in classrooms with teachers whose social competencies are low, students with socially competent teachers demonstrate higher socioemotional and academic outcomes (Jennings & Greenberg, 2009). Such teachers also have healthy relationships with their students and are more efficacious in the classroom.

SUMMARY

This final chapter reexamines many of the topics that were previously discussed in this book. This time, however, the 3 Rs and the 2 Ss are applied to you as a teacher. Multiple strategies are recommended to enhance your well-being. Because teaching is emotional, it is advantageous for teachers to accept their feelings without judging them. Instead, you are encouraged to **recognize** your own temperament and the emotions associated with it. Then examine their underlying meanings so that you can more deliberately select appropriate actions.

Although the teaching profession can be stressful, teachers differ in their reactions. Teachers who are high in negative reactivity compared to those who are low are more likely to perceive situations as stressful. Regardless of temperament, **reframing** can convert challenges into opportunities for personal or professional enhancement.

A number of advanced strategies are presented for **responding** to students with various temperaments. For example, the distress of children who are high in negative reactivity should be briefly acknowledged and then decisively redirected. In contrast, children who are high in withdrawal are sensitive and require a more gentle response.

Dilemmas encountered in the teaching profession also require a thoughtful response. Applying a problem-solving technique and possibly deliberating with others can assist you in selecting the best of the available options. Occasionally taking a "time-out" can provide a necessary respite and can positively impact your own self-regulation.

Self-care and preventive strategies **scaffold** teachers during the stressful times that could, if not averted, lead to burnout. Make healthy lifestyle choices and rely on supportive family and friends who are assets in such situations. After the difficult time has passed, it is advantageous to examine what strategies helped and which might have been beneficial if they had been applied. By regarding learning as a lifelong pursuit, you can **stretch** your knowledge base. Stretching your social competencies will benefit you as well as your students.

ASSIGNMENTS

Assignment #1: Take a Break

Learn to savor whatever discretionary time you have in order to maximize its impact. Identify several realistic ways you can take a break. Although a trip to Paris might be quite a wonderful escape, it may not be feasible. Instead, think about simple events or experiences that give you pleasure. The list of feasible pleasures is seemingly endless and can be quite inexpensive. Some of the teachers in the *INSIGHTS* program reported that taking an uninterrupted bath (with or without bubbles) in the evening can be renewing. Others reserved a particular type of coffee or tea or listened to a favorite CD or read a novel. Meeting a friend for lunch or watching a movie were other popular time-outs for pleasure. Think of a few pleasurable events or experiences. Keep your ideas realistic, but be creative.

1. _____
2. _____
3. _____
4. _____
5. _____

Select a particular time of the day or week for taking a break. Write it down to remind yourself to use it.

Assignment #2: A Contract with Yourself to Stretch Social Competency

1. Select one social competency skill that you would like to improve.

2. Select one person to whom you would like to direct your skill building.

3. Identify why you selected that person.

4. Identify a time when you are likely to need this skill.

5. Compliment yourself every time you meet your goal.

6. Keep a list of the times that you used this skill.

CLASS DISCUSSION

In small groups, discuss how you plan to complete Assignment 1 or Assignment 2. After a week, report back to the group: How did you take a break or how are you doing on your social competency contract?

RECOMMENDED READINGS

A novel of your choice.

REFERENCES

Bandura, A. (1997). *Self-efficacy: The exercise of control*. New York, NY: Freeman.

Bevans, K., Bradshaw, C., Miech, R., & Leaf, P. (2007). Staff- and school-level predictors of school organizational health: A multilevel analysis. *Journal of School Health*, *77*(6), 294–302. doi:10.1111/j.1746-1561.2007.00210.x

Carson, R. L., Baumgartner, J. J., Matthews, R. A., & Tsouloupas, C. N. (2010). Emotional exhaustion, absenteeism, and turnover intentions in childcare teachers examining the impact of physical activity behaviors. *Journal of Health Psychology*, *15*(6), 905–914. doi:10.1177/1359105309360697

Chess, S., & Thomas, A. (1984). *Origins and evolution of behavior disorders*. Cambridge, MA: Harvard University Press.

Chester, M. D., & Beaudin, B. Q. (1996). Efficacy beliefs of newly hired teachers in urban schools. *American Educational Research Journal, 99*(1), 233–257. doi:10.3102/0002831 2033001233

Chetty, R., Friedman, J. N., & Rockoff, J. E. (2011). The long-term impacts of teachers: Teacher value-added and student outcomes in adulthood. National Bureau of Economic Research, Inc., NBER Working Papers: 17699.

Helsing, D. (2007). Regarding uncertainty in teachers and teaching. *Teaching and Teacher Education, 23*, 1317–1333. doi:10.1016/j.tate.2006.06.007

Jennings, P. A., & Greenberg, M. T. (2009). The prosocial classroom: Teacher social and emotional competence in relation to student and classroom outcomes. *Review of Educational Research, 79*(1), 491–525. doi:10.3102/0034654308325693

Kokkinos, C. M., Panayiotou, G., & Davazoglou, A. M. (2005). Correlates of teacher appraisals of student behaviors. *Psychology in the Schools, 42*, 79–89. doi:10.1002/pits.20031

Lazarus, R. S., & Folkman, S. (1984). *Stress, appraisal, and coping.* New York, NY: Springer Publishing Company.

Maslach, C., & Jackson, S. E. (1981). The measurement of experienced burnout. *Journal of Organizational Behavior, 2*(2), 99–113. doi:10.1002/job.4030020205

McCarthy, C. J., Lambert, R. G., O'Donnell, M., & Melendres, L. T. (2009). The relation of elementary teachers' experience, stress, and coping resources to burnout symptom. *Elementary School Journal, 109*(3), 282–300. doi:10.1086/592308

Montgomery, C., & Rupp, A. A. (2005). A meta-analysis for exploring the diverse causes and effects of stress in teachers. *Canadian Journal of Education, 28*(3), 458–486. doi: 10.2307/4126479

Schwarzer, R., & Hallum, S. (2008). Perceived teacher self-efficacy as a predictor of job stress and burnout: Mediation analyses. *Applied Psychology, 57*(s1), 152–171. doi:10.1111/j.1464-0597.2008.00359.x

Sutton, R. E., Mudrey-Camino, R., & Knight, C. C. (2009). Teachers' emotion regulation and classroom management. *Theory Into Practice, 48*(2), 130–137. doi:10.1080/00405840 902776418

Van Kleef, G. A., Homan, A. C., & Cheshin, A. (2012). Emotional influence at work: Take it easy. *Organizational Psychology Review, 2*(4), 311–339. doi:10.1177/2041386612454911

Yoon, K. S., Duncan, T., Lee, S. W.-Y., Scarloss, B., & Shapley, K. (2007). *Reviewing the evidence on how teacher professional development affects student achievement* (Issues & Answers Report, REL 2007–No. 033). Washington, DC: U.S. Department of Education, Institute of Education Sciences, National Center for Education Evaluation and Regional Assistance, Regional Educational Laboratory Southwest.

INDEX

ABOUT THE AUTHOR

Sandee Graham McClowry, PhD, RN, FAAN, is a professor of counseling and teaching and learning in the Steinhardt School of Culture, Education, and Human Development at New York University. Dr. McClowry has conducted research in the New York City public schools for more than twenty years. She is the developer of the comprehensive evidenced-based school intervention for teachers and students and their parents called *INSIGHTS into Children's Temperament*. Dr. McClowry has received over $8 million in funding from the Institute of Education Sciences and the National Institutes of Health to test the efficacy of *INSIGHTS*. She is the past chair of the Classroom Management Special Interest Group of the American Educational Research Association.